How to Make a Texas Will

Third Edition

Karen Ann Rolcik
Mark Warda
Attorneys at Law

SPHINX® PUBLISHING
AN IMPRINT OF SOURCEBOOKS, INC.®
NAPERVILLE, ILLINOIS
www.SphinxLegal.com

Copyright © 1994, 1998, 2002 by Karen Ann Rolcik and Mark Warda
Cover and internal design © 2002 by Sourcebooks, Inc.®

All rights reserved. No part of this book may be reproduced in any form or by any electronic or mechanical means including information storage and retrieval systems—except in the case of brief quotations embodied in critical articles or reviews—without permission in writing from its publisher, Sourcebooks, Inc. Purchasers of the book are granted license to use the forms contained herein for their own personal use. No claim of copyright is made to any government form reproduced herein.

Third edition, 2002

Published by: **Sphinx® Publishing, A Imprint of Sourcebooks, Inc.®**

<u>Naperville Office</u>
P.O. Box 4410
Naperville, Illinois 60567-4410
(630) 961-3900
Fax: 630-961-2168
www.sourcebooks.com
www.SphinxLegal.com

This publication is designed to provide accurate and authoritative information in regard to the subject matter covered. It is sold with the understanding that the publisher is not engaged in rendering legal, accounting, or other professional service. If legal advice or other expert assistance is required, the services of a competent professional person should be sought.

From a Declaration of Principles Jointly Adopted by a Committee of the American Bar Association and a Committee of Publishers and Associations

This product is not a substitute for legal advice.

Disclaimer required by Texas statutes.

Library of Congress Cataloging-in-Publication Data
Rolcik, Karen Ann.
    How to make a Texas will/Karen Ann Rolcik, Mark Warda.-- 3rd ed.
        p. cm -- (Legal survival guides)
    Includes index.
    ISBN 1-57248-255-9 (alk. paper)
        1. Wills--Texas--Popular works. 2. Inheritance and succession--Texas--Popular works.
    I. Warda, Mark. II. Title. III. Series.

KFT1344.Z9 R65 2002
346.76405'4--dc21
                                                                      2002030287

Printed and bound in the United States of America.

VHG Paperback — 10 9 8 7 6 5 4 3 2 1

Contents

How a Will Is Used

Joint Tenancy

Tenancy in Common

Community Property

I/T/F Accounts

Your Homestead

Exempt Property

Automatic Changes to Your Will

Debts

Estate and Inheritance Taxes

Annual Exclusion

What a Will Can Do

Dying Without a Will

Out-of-State Wills

Who Can Make a Texas Will

What a Will Cannot Do

Who Can Use a Simple Will

Who Should Not Use a Simple Will

Using Self-Help Law Books

Before using a self-help law book, you should realize the advantages and disadvantages of doing your own legal work and understand the challenges and diligence that this requires.

THE GROWING TREND

Rest assured that you won't be the first or only person handling your own legal matter. For example, in some states, more than seventy-five percent of divorces and other cases have at least one party representing him or herself. Because of the high cost of legal services, this is a major trend and many courts are struggling to make it easier for people to represent themselves. However, some courts are not happy with people who do not use attorneys and refuse to help them in any way. For some, the attitude is, "Go to the law library and figure it out for yourself."

We at Sphinx write and publish self-help law books to give people an alternative to the often complicated and confusing legal books found in most law libraries. We have made the explanations of the law as simple and easy to understand as possible. Of course, unlike an attorney advising an individual client, we cannot cover every conceivable possibility.

COST/VALUE ANALYSIS

Whenever you shop for a product or service, you are faced with various levels of quality and price. In deciding what product or service to buy, you make a cost/value analysis on the basis of your willingness to pay and the quality you desire.

When buying a car, you decide whether you want transportation, comfort, status, or sex appeal. Accordingly, you decide among such choices as a Neon, a Lincoln, a Rolls Royce, or a Porsche. Before making a decision, you usually weigh the merits of each option against the cost.

When you get a headache, you can take a pain reliever (such as aspirin) or visit a medical specialist for a neurological examination. Given this choice, most people, of course, take a pain reliever, since it costs only pennies; whereas a medical examination costs hundreds of dollars and takes a lot of time. This is usually a logical choice because it is rare to need anything more than a pain reliever for a headache. But in some cases, a headache may indicate a brain tumor and failing to see a specialist right away can result in complications. Should everyone with a headache go to a specialist? Of course not, but people treating their own illnesses must realize that they are betting on the basis of their cost/value analysis of the situation. They are taking the most logical option.

The same cost/value analysis must be made when deciding to do one's own legal work. Many legal situations are very straight forward, requiring a simple form and no complicated analysis. Anyone with a little intelligence and a book of instructions can handle the matter without outside help.

But there is always the chance that complications are involved that only an attorney would notice. To simplify the law into a book like this, several legal cases often must be condensed into a single sentence or paragraph. Otherwise, the book would be several hundred pages long and too complicated for most people. However, this simplification necessarily leaves out many details and nuances that would apply to special or unusual situations. Also, there are many ways to interpret most legal questions. Your case may come before a judge who disagrees with the analysis of our authors.

Therefore, in deciding to use a self-help law book and to do your own legal work, you must realize that you are making a cost/value analysis. You have decided that the money you will save in doing it yourself outweighs the chance that your case will not turn out to your satisfaction. Most people handling their own simple legal matters never have a problem, but occasionally people find that it ended up costing them more to have an attorney straighten out the situation than it would have if they had hired an attorney in the beginning. Keep this in mind if you decide to handle your own case, and be sure to consult an attorney if you feel you might need further guidance.

LOCAL RULES   The next thing to remember is that a book that covers the law for the entire nation, or even for an entire state, cannot possibly include every procedural difference of every county court. Whenever possible, we provide the exact form needed; however, in some areas, each county, or even each judge, may require unique forms and procedures. In our *state* books, our forms usually cover the majority of counties in the state, or provide examples of the type of form that will be required. In our *national* books, our forms are sometimes even more general in nature but are designed to give a good idea of the type of form that will be needed in most locations. Nonetheless, keep in mind that your *state*, county, or judge may have a requirement, or use a form, that is not included in this book.

You should not necessarily expect to be able to get all of the information and resources you need solely from within the pages of this book. This book will serve as your guide, giving you specific information whenever possible and helping you to find out what else you will need to know. This is just like if you decided to build your own backyard deck. You might purchase a book on how to build decks. However, such a book would not include the building codes and permit requirements of every city, town, county, and township in the nation; nor would it include the lumber, nails, saws, hammers, and other materials and tools you would need to actually build the deck. You would use the book as your guide, and then do some work and research involving such matters as whether you need a permit of some kind, what type and grade of wood are available in your area, whether to use hand tools or power tools, and how to use those tools.

Before using the forms in a book like this, you should check with your court clerk to see if there are any local rules of which you should be aware, or local forms you will need to use. Often, such forms will require the same information as the forms in the book but are merely laid out differently, use slightly different language, or use different color paper so the clerks can easily find them. They will sometimes require additional information.

CHANGES IN THE LAW

Besides being subject to state and local rules and practices, the law is subject to change at any time. The courts and the legislatures of all fifty states are constantly revising the laws. It is possible that while you are reading this book, some aspect of the law is being changed or a court is interpreting a law in a different way. You should always check the most recent statutes, rules and regulations to see what, if any changes have been made.

In most cases, the change will be of minimal significance. A form will be redesigned, additional information will be required, or a waiting period will be extended. As a result, you might need to revise a form, file an extra form, or wait out a longer time period; these types of changes will not usually affect the outcome of your case. On the other hand, sometimes a major part of the law is changed, the entire law in a particular area is rewritten, or a case that was the basis of a central legal point is overruled. In such instances, your entire ability to pursue your case may be impaired.

Again, you should weigh the value of your case against the cost of an attorney and make a decision as to what you believe is in your best interest.

INTRODUCTION

This book was written to help Texas residents quickly and easily make their own wills without the expense or delay of hiring a lawyer. It begins with a short explanation of how a will works and what a will can and cannot do. It is designed to allow those with simple estates to quickly and inexpensively set up their affairs to distribute their property according to their wishes. It includes an explanation of how such things as joint property and *pay on death* accounts will affect your planning.

It also includes information on appointing a guardian for any minor children you may have. This will help you to avoid bad feelings between relatives and to protect the children from being raised by someone you would object to.

Chapters 1 through 10 explain the laws that affect the making of a will. Appendix B contains sample filled-in forms to show you how it is done. Appendix C contains blank will forms you can use. A flow chart in Appendix C will help you choose the right will form based upon your circumstances and desires.

You can prepare your own will quickly and easily by using the forms out of the book, by photocopying them, or by retyping the material on sheets of paper. The small amount of time it takes to do this can give you and your loved ones the peace of mind of knowing that your estate will be distributed according to your wishes.

A surprising number of people have had their estates pass to the wrong parties because of a simple lack of knowledge of how the laws work. Before using any of the forms in Appendix C, you should read and understand all of this book.

In each example given in the text you might ask, "What if the spouse died first?" or "What if the children were grown up?" and the solution might change because of your question. If your situation is at all complicated, you should seek the advice of an attorney. In many communities, wills are available for very reasonable prices. No book of this type can cover every contingency in every case, but a knowledge of the basics will help you to make the right decisions regarding your property.

The forms in this book are designed to leave property to your family, or if you have no family, to friends or charities. As will be explained in Chapter 2, if you wish to disinherit your family and leave your property to others, you should consult with an attorney who can be sure that your will cannot be successfully challenged in court.

Overview 1

A *will* is a document you can use to control who gets your property; who will be guardian of your children and their property; and, who will manage your estate upon your death.

Before making your will, you should understand how a will works and what it can and cannot do. Otherwise, your plans may not be carried out and the wrong people may end up with your property.

How a Will Is Used

Some people think a will avoids *probate*, when in fact it does not. A will is the document used in probate to determine who receives the property and who is appointed guardian and executor or personal representative.

AVOIDING PROBATE

If you wish to avoid probate, you need to use methods other than a will, such as joint ownership, pay-on-death accounts, or living trusts. The first two of these are discussed later in this chapter.

If a person successfully avoids probate with all of his or her property, then he or she may not need a will. In most cases, when a husband or wife dies, no will or probate is necessary because everything is jointly owned. However, everyone should have a will in case some property that one forgets to put into joint ownership or that one receives just prior to death does not avoid probate for some reason, or in case both husband and wife die in the same accident.

Joint Tenancy

PROBATE   Property that is owned in *joint tenancy with right of survivorship* does not pass in a will and does not go through probate. It automatically passes to the joint owner upon the death of the co-owner. You only need to provide a death certificate to change the title and remove the decedent's name from ownership.

However, there are exceptions to this rule. If money is put into a joint account only for convenience, it might pass through the will; but if the joint owner refuses to give the money away, it could take an expensive court battle to get it back.

Putting property into joint tenancy does not give the recipient absolute rights to it. If the estate owes estate taxes, the recipient of joint tenancy property may have to contribute to the tax payment. Also, if property is deemed to be *community property*, it may pass to the spouse rather than the joint owner.

Example 1:   Ted and his wife, Michelle, want all of their property to go to each other, if one dies before the other. They put their house, cars, bank accounts, and brokerage accounts in joint ownership. When Ted dies, Michelle only has to show his death certificate to get all the property transferred to her name. No probate or will is necessary.

Example 2:   After Ted's death, Michelle, puts all of the property and accounts into joint ownership with her son, Mark. Upon Michelle's death, Mark needs only to present her death certificate to have everything transferred into his name. No probate or will is necessary.

YOUR WILL   It is most simple if all property is in joint ownership or if all property is distributed through a will. But when some property is distributed through each method, a person's plans may not be fulfilled.

Example 1:   Bill's will leaves all his property to his sister, Mary. Bill dies owning a house jointly with his wife, Joan, and a bank account jointly with his son, Don. Upon Bill's death, Joan gets the house, Don gets the bank account, and Mary gets nothing.

Example 2:   Betty's will leaves half her assets to her sister, Ann, and half her assets to her husband, George. Betty dies owning $1,000,000 in stock jointly with George, and a car in her name alone. Ann gets only a half interest in the car. George gets all the stock and a half interest in the car.

Example 3:   John's will leaves all his property equally to his five children. Before going in the hospital, he puts his oldest son, Harry, as a joint owner of his accounts. John dies and Harry gets all of his assets. The rest of the children get nothing.

In each of these cases, the property went to a person it probably shouldn't have because the decedent didn't realize that joint ownership overruled his or her will. In some families, this might not be a problem. Harry might divide the property equally. But Harry might also keep everything, and the family would never talk to him again, or would take him to court.

NOTE: *By* joint tenancy *and* joint ownership *we are referring to "JTWROS." On a bank account, this would be designated "OR." If the property were to be titled as "tenants in common" ("AND"), then one-half of the property would go to the joint owner and one-half would pass under the will.*

RISKS In many cases, joint property can be an ideal way to own property and avoid probate. However, it does have risks. If you put your real estate in joint ownership with someone, you cannot sell it or mortgage it without that person's signature. If you put your bank account in joint ownership with someone, they can withdraw your money.

Example 1: Alice put her house in joint ownership with her son. She later married Ed and moved in with him. She wanted to sell her house and invest the money for income. Her son refused to sign the deed because he wanted to keep the home in the family. She was in court for ten months getting her house back and the judge almost refused to do it.

Example 2: Alex put his bank accounts into joint ownership with his daughter, Mary, to avoid probate. Mary fell in love with Doug, who was in trouble with the law. Doug talked Mary into "borrowing" $30,000 from the account for a business deal that went sour. Later she "borrowed" $25,000 more to pay Doug's bail bond. Alex didn't find out until it was too late, and his money was gone.

TENANCY IN COMMON

There are two basic ways to own property: joint tenancy with right of survivorship and tenancy in common. As explained earlier, *joint tenancy with right of survivorship* means that if one owner of the property dies, the survivor automatically gets the decedent's share. *Tenancy in common* means when one owner dies, that owner's share of the property goes to his or her heirs or beneficiaries under the will. People use tenancy in common if they do not want the co-owner to inherit their share.

Example: Tom and Marcia bought a house and lived together for twenty years, but were never married. The deed did not specify joint tenancy. When Tom died, his brother inherited his half of the house, and it had to be sold because Marcia could not afford to buy it from him.

Community Property

Under Texas law, property possessed by either spouse during a marriage is characterized as *community property* or *separate property*. Separate property is property owned by a spouse before marriage, property acquired during the marriage by gift or inheritance, and funds recovered by a spouse for personal injuries. All other property acquired during the marriage is community property. Each spouse automatically owns a half interest in the community property, and his or her will only controls that spouse's half interest.

Example 1: Mark and Barb have been married for several years. During their marriage, Barb stays at home to raise the children. Their stocks and bank accounts are only in Mark's name. Mark's will leaves all his property to his sister, Liz, and nothing to his wife. Barb gets half of all property that the court designates as *community property*. Liz gets the other half of the community property and all of Mark's separate property.

Example 2: Bill and Jane are married, and both work. Prior to their marriage, Jane saved $5,000 and kept this property in a separate account. While they are married, Jane's parents die leaving her $20,000. Jane's will leaves all her property to her brother, Derk. Derk gets the $25,000 of separate property and Jane's half of the community property. Bill keeps his half of the community property. Derk, however, gets only half of the income that was earned by the $25,000, because under Texas law, income earned by separate property is community property.

I/T/F ACCOUNTS

BANK
ACCOUNTS

One way to keep bank accounts out of your estate and still retain control is to title them *in trust for* (I/T/F), which means you can name a beneficiary.

NOTE: *Some banks may call it pay on death (POD) or transfer on death (TOD).*

With I/T/F bank accounts, no one except you can use the money until your death, and then it immediately goes directly to the person you name, without a will or probate proceeding. These bank accounts are sometimes called *Totten trusts* after the court case that declared them legal.

Example: Rich opened a bank account in the name of "Rich, I/T/F Mary." If Rich dies, the money automatically goes to Mary. Prior to his death, Mary has no control over the account, and in fact, does not even have to know about it. So Rich can take Mary's name off the account at any time.

SECURITIES AND
MUTUAL FUNDS

A law has been passed by many states that allows people to register their stock, bonds, mutual funds and other securities in the I/T/F form. If you own these types of investments you can keep them out of probate by using this method.

Unfortunately, Texas has not yet passed this law, but you can take advantage of it. If your mutual fund or brokerage account is with a company in one of the states that allows such registrations, you can set up an I/T/F account. If the broker or mutual fund cannot offer I/T/F accounts, it may be worth changing to a state that does.

YOUR HOMESTEAD

There are two meanings for the word *homestead* in Texas. In one sense, a homestead is the tax exemption that you get from the property appraiser when you reside on a property. In another sense, it means a homestead for estate purposes, which is property that is the permanent residence of a legal resident of Texas.

If your property is homestead in the second sense, your will cannot destroy the rights of your surviving spouse and minor children to the homestead. Your surviving spouse has the right to live in the homestead for the rest of his or her life, no matter who you give it to under your will. Upon the surviving spouse's death, or when the surviving spouse no longer uses it as a homestead, the homestead passes to the people named in your will.

If you have minor children but no spouse, the children have the right to live in the homestead for as long as necessary. After a court determines it is no longer necessary to use the homestead, it passes to the people named in your will.

Example 1: John's will leaves his homestead to his adult children from his previous marriage and the rest of his property to his wife, Dawn. Upon his death, Dawn gets all of his property and the right to live in the homestead for the rest of her life or until she moves to another house. Upon her death or when she moves, the children get the homestead.

Example 2: Margaret is a widow with two minor children. In her will, she leaves her homestead to her parents and the rest of her property to her children. The children have the right to use the homestead until they reach age eighteen and are able to support themselves. When both of the children can support themselves, Margaret's parents get the homestead.

EXEMPT PROPERTY

If you have a spouse or minor children, then up to $30,000 in "household furniture, furnishings, and appliances" in your "usual place of abode" and all automobiles in your name that are regularly used by you or members of your family are exempt from your will. This property is called *exempt property.* If you have a spouse, your spouse gets this property; if you have no spouse, your children receive it. Additionally, a spouse or minor children may receive a *family allowance* of an amount deemed reasonable by the court to defray living expenses during the first year following the death.

Example: Donna dies and her will gives half her property to her husband and half to her grown son from a previous marriage. Donna's property consists of a $5,000 automobile, $5,000 in furniture, and $5,000 cash. Donna's husband may be able to get the car and the furniture as exempt property, and the $5,000 as a family allowance—leaving nothing for the son.

To avoid having property declared exempt, you may specifically give it to someone in a will. If cash is kept in a joint or I/T/F bank account, it goes to the joint owner or beneficiary and cannot be used as the family allowance.

AUTOMATIC CHANGES TO YOUR WILL

MARRIAGE   If you get married after you make your will and you do not rewrite it after the wedding, your spouse gets a share of your estate as if you had no will. The only exceptions are if you have a pre-nuptial agreement; you made a provision for your spouse in the will; or, if you stated in the will that you intended not to mention your spouse.

Example: John wrote his will leaving everything to his physically-challenged brother. When he married Joan, who had plenty of money, he did not change his will because he still wanted his brother to get his estate. When he died, Joan received her half of the community property and John's brother received the other half of the community property.

DIVORCE
If you get divorced after making your will and do not rewrite it after the divorce is finalized, all provisions for your spouse in the will are void, including the nomination of the spouse as trustee of any property you leave to your children.

Example: Mark and Barb execute wills during their marriage leaving two-thirds of their property to each other and one-third in trust to their children. Mark and Barb are named executors of each other's wills and trustees of the children's trust. After their divorce, all provisions leaving property to each other and the nominations as executor and trustee are void.

If you intend to allow your former spouse to act as trustee of the children's trust, you must make a new will or make a *codicil* (an amendment to a will) it after the date on which the divorce is final.

CHILDREN
If you have a child after making your will and do not rewrite it, the child may receive a share of your estate, as if there was no will.

Example: Dave made a will leaving half his estate to his sister and the other half to be shared by his three children. He later had another child and did not revise his will. Upon his death, his sister received half of the estate and the children received one-eighth each.

It is best to rewrite your will at the birth of a child. However, another solution is to include the following clause after the names of your children in your will:

"...and any afterborn children living at the time of my death, in equal shares."

If you have children but are leaving all of your property to your spouse, then your will is not affected by the birth of a subsequent child.

DEBTS

One of the duties of the person administering an estate is to pay the debts of the decedent. Before an estate is distributed, the legitimate debts must be ascertained and paid.

An exception is *secured debts*, which are protected by a lien against property, like a home loan or a car loan. In the case of a secured debt, the loan does not have to be paid before the property is distributed.

Example: John owns a $100,000 house with an $80,000 mortgage, and he has $100,000 in the bank. If he leaves the house to his brother and the bank account to his sister, then his brother receives the home, but owes the $80,000 mortgage.

What if your debts are more than your property? Today, unlike hundreds of years ago, people cannot inherit other peoples' debts. A person's property is used to pay his or her probate and funeral expenses first, and if there is not enough left to pay the other debts, then the creditors are out of luck. However, if a person leaves property to someone and does not have enough assets to pay his or her debts, then the property will be sold to pay the debts.

Example: Jeb's will leaves all of his property to his three children. At the time of his death, Jeb has $30,000 in medical bills, $11,000 in credit card debt, and his only assets are his car and $5,000 in stock. The car and stock are sold and the funeral bill and probate fees are paid out of the proceeds. If any money is left, it goes to the creditors, and nothing is left for the children. The children do not have to pay the medical bills or credit card debt.

ESTATE AND INHERITANCE TAXES

Unlike some states, Texas does not have an independent estate or inheritance tax. The only time estate taxes are paid to the state of Texas is if the estate is subject to federal estate taxes and a credit is allowed for state taxes. The amount of the credit is paid to the state of Texas.

There is a federal estate tax for estates worth above a certain amount. Estates worth below that amount are allowed a *unified credit*, which exempts them from tax. The *unified credit* determines the amount of property a person can leave at his or her death or give away during his or her lifetime without paying tax to the Internal Revenue Service. In 2002 and 2003, the amount of property exempted by the unified credit is $1,000,000 but it will rise to $3,500,000 by the year 2009. In 2010, there will be no estate tax. However, as the law is now written, in 2011 the federal estate tax will return and the amount of exempted property will be $1,000,000. The amount will change according to the following schedule.

Year	Unified Credit Amount
2002	$1,000,000
2003	$1,000,000
2004	$1,500,000
2005	$1,500,000
2006	$2,000,000
2007	$2,000,000
2008	$2,000,000
2009	$3,500,000
2010	N/A

Annual Exclusion

When a person makes a gift, that gift is subtracted from the amount entitled to the unified credit available to his or her estate at death. However, a person is allowed to make gifts of up to $10,000 per person per year without having these gifts subtracted from the unified credit. This means a married couple can make gifts of up to $20,000 per person. The Taxpayer Relief Act of 1997 provided that this exclusion amount will be adjusted for inflation.

NEEDING A TEXAS WILL 2

WHAT A WILL CAN DO

BENEFICIARIES

A will allows you to decide who will be a *beneficiary*—the person who inherits your property after your death. You can give specific personal items to certain persons and choose which people, if any, deserve a greater share of your estate. You can also leave gifts to schools and charities.

EXECUTOR

A will allows you to determine an *executor*—the person who will be in charge of handling your estate. This person gathers all your assets and distributes them to the beneficiaries, hires attorneys or accountants if necessary, and files any essential tax or probate forms. You can provide in a will that your executor does not have to post a surety bond with the court in order to serve, which can save your estate some money. You can also give him or her the power to sell your property and take other actions without a court order.

GUARDIAN

A will allows you to choose a *guardian*—a person to raise your minor children. This way you can avoid fights among relatives and make sure the best person raises your children. You may also appoint separate guardians over your children and their money. For example, you may appoint your sister as guardian over your children and your father as guardian over their money. That way, a second person can provide input on how the children's money is spent.

PROTECTING
HEIRS

You can set up a trust to provide that your property is not distributed immediately. Many people feel that their children would not be ready to handle large sums of money at the *age of majority*, which is age eighteen. A will can direct the money to be held until the children are twenty-one, twenty-five, or older.

MINIMIZING
TAXES

If your estate is over the amount protected by the federal *unified credit* ($1,000,000, but phased out completely by the year 2010) then it will be subject to federal estate taxes. If you wish to lower those taxes, by making gifts to charities, for example, you can do so through a will. However, such estate planning is beyond the scope of this book and you should consult an estate planning attorney or another book for further information.

INDEPENDENT
ESTATE
ADMINISTRATION

By including special language in your will, you can provide that your executor is an *independent executor*, which means he or she is independent of court supervision. This saves a great deal of time and money because it frees your executor from filing lots of paperwork with the court and from having to first obtain the court's permission before handling estate matters as they arise, which is required in a dependent estate administration.

DYING WITHOUT A WILL

If you do not have a will, Texas law dictates how your property will be distributed. The law will distinguish between separate and community property and distribute each as follows:

- If you leave a spouse and no children, your spouse gets all of your separate personal property, all of your community property, and half of your separate *real property*. The other half of the real property goes to either your parents, your brothers and sisters (or their children), your grandparents, or your aunts and uncles (or their children).

- If you leave a spouse and children, your spouse gets ownership of half of all community property and one-third of your separate personal property. Your children get ownership of half of all community property, two-thirds of your separate personal property, and all of your separate real property. Your spouse has the right, however, to share the benefits from one-third of your separate real property. (These benefits commonly are the right to live on the property.)

- If you leave children and no spouse, all of your children get equal shares of your estate.

- If you leave no spouse *and* no children, then your estate goes to the living people highest on the following list:

  - your parents;

  - your brothers and sisters (or if dead, their children);

  - your grandparents; and,

  - your uncles and aunts or their children.

OUT-OF-STATE WILLS

A will that is valid in another state is probably valid to pass property in Texas. However, before such a will can be accepted by a Texas Probate Court, a person in your former state has to be appointed as a *foreign executor* to take the oath of a person who witnessed your signature on the will. Because of the expense and delay of having a foreign executor appointed and the problem of finding out-of-state witnesses, it is advised that you execute a new will after moving to Texas.

Another advantage to having a Texas will is that as a Texas resident, your estate will pay no state probate or inheritance taxes. If you move to Texas but keep your old will, your former state of residence may try to collect taxes on your estate.

Texas also allows a will to be *self-proved*, which means that witnesses never have to be called in to take an oath. With special self-proving language in your will, the witnesses take the oath at the time of signing and never have to be seen again. Also, a Texas will allows you to make your executor an *independent executor* saving your estate a lot of time and expense.

Example: George and Barbara left their high-tax state and retired to Texas, but they never made a new will. Upon their deaths, their former state of residence tried to collect a tax from their estate because their wills stated that they were residents of that state.

WHO CAN MAKE A TEXAS WILL

Any person who is eighteen years of age and of sound mind can make a valid will in Texas.

WHAT A WILL CANNOT DO

A will cannot direct that anything illegal be done, and it cannot put unreasonable conditions on a gift. A provision that your daughter receives all of your property if she divorces her husband would be ignored by the court. She would get the property with no conditions attached. You can put some conditions in your will, but be sure they are enforceable by consulting an attorney.

A will cannot leave money or property to an animal because animals cannot legally own property. If you wish to continue paying for the care of an animal after your death, you should leave the funds in a trust or to a friend whom you know will care for the animal.

WHO CAN USE A SIMPLE WILL

The wills in this book will pass your estate whether it is $1,000 or $100,000,000. However, if your estate is over $1,000,000, then you might be able to avoid estate taxes by using a trust or other tax-saving device. The larger your estate, the more you can save on estate taxes by doing more complicated planning. If you have a large estate and are concerned about estate taxes, you should consult an estate planning attorney or a book on estate planning.

WHO SHOULD NOT USE A SIMPLE WILL

CONTESTED WILL
If you expect that there may be a fight over your estate or that someone might contest your will's validity, then you should consult a lawyer. If you leave one or more of your children out of your will, it is likely that someone will contest your will.

COMPLICATED ESTATES
If you are the beneficiary of a trust or have any complications in your legal relationships, such as children from more than one marriage and a second spouse, you may need special provisions in your will.

BLIND OR UNABLE TO WRITE
A person who is blind or who can sign only with an "X" should also consult a lawyer about the proper way to make and execute a will.

ESTATES OVER $1,000,000
If you expect to have over $1,000,000 at the time of your death, you may want to consult with a CPA or tax attorney regarding tax consequences.

CONDITIONS
If you wish to put some sort of conditions or restrictions on the property you leave, you should consult a lawyer. For example, if you want to leave money to your brother only if he quits smoking, or to a hospital only if they name a wing in your honor, you should consult an attorney to be sure that your conditions are valid.

How to Make a Simple Will 3

Identifying Parties in Your Will

PEOPLE

When making your will, it is important to clearly identify the people you name as your beneficiaries. In some families, names differ only by middle initial or by Jr. or Sr. Be sure to check everyone's name before making your will. You can also add your relationship to the beneficiary and their location, such as "my cousin, Maxine Martindale of Austin, Texas."

ORGANIZATIONS

The same applies to organizations and charities. For example, more than one group uses the words "cancer society" or "heart association" in their name. Be sure to get the correct name of the group that you intend to leave your gift. This can often be done by calling the organization and getting its appropriate legal name.

SPOUSE AND CHILDREN

In most states, you must mention your spouse and children in your will even if you do not leave them any property to show that you are of sound mind and know who are your heirs. As mentioned earlier, if you have a spouse and/or children and plan to leave your property to people other than them, you should consult an attorney to be sure that your will can be enforced.

PERSONAL PROPERTY

Because people acquire and dispose of personal property so often, it is not advisable to list a lot of small items in your will. Otherwise, when you sell or replace one of them you may have to rewrite your will.

One solution is to describe the type of item you wish to give, rather than the specific item. For example, instead of saying, "I leave my 1998 Ford to my sister," you should say, "I leave any automobile I own at the time of my death to my sister."

Of course, if you do mean to give a specific item, you should describe it. For example, instead of saying "I leave my diamond ring to Joan," you should say, "I leave to Joan the half carat diamond ring that I inherited from my grandmother," in case you own more than one diamond ring at the time of your death.

SPECIFIC BEQUESTS

Occasionally a person will want to leave something to a friend or charity and the rest to the family. This can be done with a *specific bequest*, such as "$1,000 to my friend Martha Jones." However, there could be a problem if, at the time of a person's death, there is not anything left after the specific bequests.

Example: At the time of making his will, Todd had $1,000,000 in assets. He felt generous, so he left $50,000 to a local hospital, $50,000 to a local group that took care of homeless animals, and the rest to his children. Unfortunately, at the time of his death, his estate was worth only $110,000, so after the above specific bequests, the legal fees, and the expenses of probate, there was nothing left for his children.

Another problem with specific bequests is that some of the property might be worth considerably more or less at death than when the will was made.

Example: Joe wanted his two children to share his estate equally. His will left his son his stocks (worth $500,000 at the time) and his daughter $500,000 in cash. By the time of Joe's death the stock was only worth $100,000.

He should have left fifty percent of his estate to each child. It is common to list percentages for each beneficiary so that if your property changes over the years, it will still be divided fairly. If giving certain things to certain people is an important part of your estate plan, you can do it, but remember to change your will if your assets change.

JOINT
BENEFICIARIES

Be careful about leaving one item of personal property to more than one person. For example, if you leave something to your son and his wife, what happens if they divorce? Even if you leave something to two of your own children, what if they cannot agree about who will have possession of it? Whenever possible, leave property to only one person.

REMAINDER CLAUSE

One of the most important clauses in a will is the *remainder clause* (sometimes called the *residue clause*). This is the clause that says something like "all the rest of my property I leave to…" This clause ensures that the will disposes of all property owned at the time of death that is not given away by a specific bequest so that nothing is forgotten.

In a simple will, the best way to distribute property is to put it all in the remainder clause. In the first example in the previous section, the problem would have been avoided if the will had read as follows: "The rest, residue, and remainder of my estate I leave, five percent to ABC Hospital, five percent to XYZ Animal Welfare League and ninety percent to be divided equally among my children…"

ALTERNATE BENEFICIARIES

You should always provide for an *alternate beneficiary*, or a person who will inherit your estate in case the person you name dies before you, and you do not have a chance to make out a new will.

SURVIVOR OR
DESCENDANTS

Suppose your will leaves your property to your sister and brother but your brother predeceases you. Should his share go to your sister or to your brother's children or grandchildren? If you are giving property to two or more people and you want it all to go to the other if one of them dies, then you must specify "or the survivor of them."

If, on the other hand, you want the property to go to the children of the deceased person, you should state in your will, "or their lineal descendants." This includes his or her children and grandchildren.

FAMILY OR
PERSON

If you decide you want it to go to your brother's children and grandchildren, you must also decide if an equal share should go to each family or to each person. For example, if your brother leaves three grandchildren, and one is an only child of his daughter and the others are the children of his son, should all grandchildren get equal shares or should they split their parent's share?

When you want each family to get an equal share it is called *per stirpes*. When you want each person to get an equal share it is called *per capita*. Most of the wills in this book use per stirpes because that is the most common way property is left. If you wish to leave your property per capita then you can rewrite the will with this change.

Example: Alice leaves her property to her two daughters, Mary and Pat, in equal shares, or to their lineal descendants per stirpes. Both daughters die before Alice. Mary leaves one child; Pat leaves two children. In this case Mary's child gets half of the estate and Pat's children split the other half of the estate. If Alice had specified per capita instead of per stirpes, then each child would have gotten one-third of the estate.

Per Stirpes Distribution

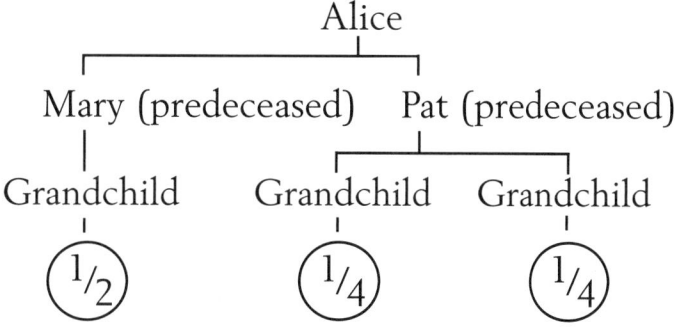

Per Capita Distribution

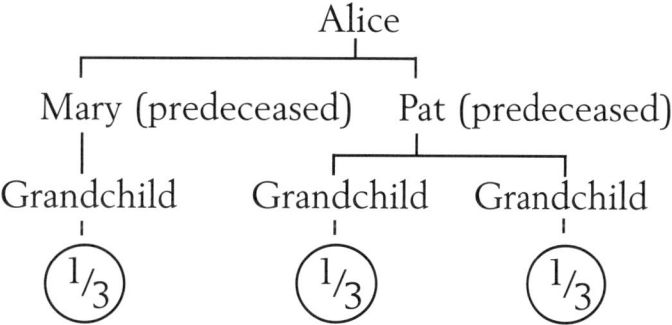

There are fourteen different will forms in this book that should cover the options most people want, but you may want to divide your property slightly differently from what is stated in these forms. If so, you can retype the forms according to your wishes, specifying whether the property should go to the survivor or the lineal descendants. If you have any questions, you should seek the advice of an attorney.

SURVIVORSHIP

Many people put a clause in their will stating that anyone receiving property under the will must survive for thirty, forty-five, or sixty days after the death of the person who made the will. This provision is so that if the two people die in the same accident, there will not be two probates, and the property will not go to the other party's heirs.

Example: Fred and Wilma were married and each had children by previous marriages. They did not have survivorship clauses in their wills, and they were in an airplane crash and died. Fred's children hired several expert witnesses and a law firm to prove that at the time of the crash, Fred lived for a few minutes longer than Wilma. So, when Wilma died first, all of her property went to Fred. When he died a few minutes later, all of Fred *and* Wilma's property went to his children. Wilma's children got nothing.

GUARDIANS

If you have minor children, you should name a guardian for them. There are two types of guardians: a guardian over the *person* and a guardian over the *property*. The guardian over the person decides where the children will live and makes the other parental decisions for them. A guardian over the property is in charge of the minor's property and inheritance. In most cases, one person is appointed guardian over both the person and property. But some people prefer the children to live with one person, but to have the money held by another person.

Example: Sandra was a widow with a young daughter. She knew that if anything happened to her, her sister would be the best person to raise her daughter. But her sister was never good with money. So when Sandra wrote her will, she named her sister as guardian over the person of her daughter, and she named her father as guardian over the estate of her daughter.

When naming a guardian, it is always advisable to name an *alternate guardian*, or a person to serve as guardian in case your first choice is unable to serve for any reason.

Children's Trust

When a parent dies leaving a minor child, and the child's property is held by a guardian, in Texas the guardianship ends when the child reaches the age of eighteen. At that point, all of the property is turned over to the child. Most parents do not feel their children are competent at the age of eighteen to handle large sums of money and prefer that it be held until the child is twenty-one, twenty-five, thirty, or even older.

If you wish to set up a system of determining when your children should receive various amounts of your estate, or if you want the property held to a higher age than thirty-five, you should consult a lawyer to draft a trust. However, if you want a simple provision that the funds be held until the children reach a higher age than eighteen, and you trust someone to make decisions about paying for education or other expenses for your child or children, you can put that provision in your will as a *children's trust*.

The children's trust trustee can be the same person as the guardian or a different person. It is advisable to name an alternate trustee in case your first choice is unable to handle the trust.

Trusts for Parents

Today it is not uncommon for a parent to live longer than his or her adult child. With the high cost of medical care, assisted living, and nursing homes, an adult child may wish to set aside some part of his or her estate in trust for the benefit of his or her parents.

If the parent is receiving Medicaid or some other form of government assistance *or* lives in a residential facility that requires all of a resident's assets be turned over to the facility for the resident's care, the child should keep property in a trust for the benefit of his or her parents. This type of planning is very complex and many state and federal rules must be followed. If you are considering such a provision for your will, you should consult an attorney who is familiar with Medicaid planning and trusts for the elderly.

Executor

An *executor* is the person who will be in charge of your probate. He or she will gather your assets, handle the sale of them if necessary, prepare an inventory, hire an attorney, and distribute the property. If this is a person you trust, then you can state in your will that no bond will be required to be posted by him or her. Otherwise, the court will require that a *surety bond* be paid for by your estate to guaranty that the person is honest. You can appoint a bank to handle your estate, but bank fees are usually very high.

It is best to appoint a resident of Texas because it is easier for them to perform their duties and because a bond might be required of a non-resident, even if your will waives the requirement.

Some people like to name two people to handle their estate to avoid jealousy or to have them check on each other's honesty. However, this makes double work in getting the papers signed and creates problems if they cannot agree on something.

WITNESSES

A will must be witnessed by two people to be valid in Texas. In all states except Vermont, only two witnesses are required, so unless you own property in Vermont, you do not need more than two witnesses.

In Texas it is legal for a beneficiary of a will to be a witness to the will. However, this can cause problems, especially if there is anyone who may contest your will.

SELF-PROVING AFFIDAVIT

As mentioned above, a will only needs two witnesses to be legal, but if it includes a *self-proving affidavit* and is notarized, then the will can be admitted to probate quickly. If the will is *not* self-proved, then one of the witnesses must testify in court and sign a sworn statement that the will is genuine.

In an emergency situation (for example, if you are bedridden and there is no notary available), you can execute your will without the self-proving affidavit. As long as it has two witnesses it will be valid. The only drawback is that at least one of the witnesses will later have to go to court, testify and sign an oath.

DISINHERITING SOMEONE

If you intend to disinherit someone, you should not make your own will (without an attorney), because it may result in your will being challenged in court. However, you may make your own will if you wish to leave one child less of your estate than another because you already made a gift to that child, or perhaps that child needs the money less than the other. If you do give more to one child than to another, then you should state your reasons to prove that you thought about your plan. Otherwise the one who receives less might argue that you did not realize what you were doing and were not competent to make a will.

FUNERAL ARRANGEMENTS

There is no harm in stating your funeral preferences in your will, but in most states, including Texas, directions for a funeral are not legally enforceable. Often a will is not found until after the funeral. Therefore it is better to tell your family about your wishes or to make prior arrangements yourself.

HANDWRITTEN WILLS

In Texas, a person can hand-write a will without any witnesses, and it will be held valid. A hand-written will is called a *holographic* will. It must be entirely in your own handwriting and clearly express your intention to make it your will.

Since there is a greater chance an unwitnessed handwritten will will be held invalid, you should only use one in an emergency, such as if you are ill and unable to locate any witnesses.

FORMS

There are more than twenty different will forms included in this book for easy use. You can either cut them out, photocopy them, or retype them on plain paper.

The forms in this book are printed on both sides of the page. If you photocopy them on separate pages or type your will on more than one piece of paper, you should staple the pages together, initial each page and have both witnesses initial each page . Each page should state at the bottom, "page 1 of 3," "page 2 of 3," etc.

CORRECTIONS

Your will should have no white-outs or erasures. If for some reason it is impossible to make a will without corrections, each correction should be initialed by you and both witnesses.

How to Execute Your Will 4

Signing a will is a serious legal event, and it must be done properly or the will can be declared invalid. Preferably, it should be done in a private room without distraction. All parties must watch each other sign, and no one should leave the area until all have signed.

Example: Ebenezer was bedridden in a small room. His will was brought in to him to sign, but the witnesses could not actually see his hand signing because a dresser was in the way. His will was ignored by the court and his property went to two people who were not in his will.

PROCEDURE   To be sure your will is valid, follow these rules:

☛ Say to your witnesses, "This is my will. I have read it, I understand it, and this is how I want it to read. I want you two (or three) people to be my witnesses." Contrary to popular belief, you do not have to read the will to the witnesses or let them read it.

☛ Date your will and sign your name at the end in ink exactly as it is printed in the will.

☛ Initial each page as both witnesses watch.

☛ Watch with the other witnesses as each party signs in ink and initials each page.

SELF-PROVING AFFIDAVIT   As explained in the last chapter, it is important to attach a self-proving affidavit to your will. You will need to have a notary public present to watch everyone sign. If it is impossible to have a notary present, your will is still valid, but the probate process might be delayed.

After your witnesses have signed as attesting witnesses under your name, you all should sign the self-proving page, and the notary should notarize it. The notary should not be one of your witnesses.

It is a good idea to make at least one copy of your will, but do not personally sign the copies or have them notarized. The reason for this is if you cancel or destroy your will, someone may produce a copy of your old will and have it probated. Also, if you lose or destroy a notarized copy, a court may assume you intended to revoke the original.

Example: Michael typed out a copy of his will and made two photocopies. He had the original and both copies signed and notarized. He then gave the original to his sister, who was his executor, and kept the two copies. Upon his death, the two copies could not be found. Because these copies were in his possession, it was assumed that he destroyed them. A court ruled that by destroying them, he must have intended to revoke the original will, and his property went to people not listed in his will.

AFTER YOU SIGN YOUR WILL 5

STORING YOUR WILL

Your will should be kept in a place safe from fire and easily accessible to your heirs. Your executor should know where it is. It can be kept in a home safe or a fire box. Also, in Texas, a will can be removed from a safe deposit box easily, so you can keep it there.

If you are close to your children and can trust them, then you can allow one of them to keep the will in his or her safe deposit box. However, if you later decide to limit that child's share, there could be a problem.

Example: Diane wrote her will giving her property to her two children equally and gave it to her older child, Bill, to hold. Years later, Bill moved away, and her younger child, Mary, took care of her every day. Diane made a new will giving most of her property to Mary. Upon Diane's death, Bill came to town and found the new will in Diane's house. He destroyed it and probated the old will, which gave him half the property.

REVOKING YOUR WILL

The usual way to revoke a will is to execute a new one that states that it revokes all previously made wills. To revoke a will without making a new one, you can tear, burn, cancel, deface, obliterate, or destroy it, as long as you do this with the intention of revoking it. If it is destroyed accidentally, the will is not legally revoked.

Example: Ralph tells his son, Clyde, to go to the basement safe to tear up his (Ralph's) will. However, if Clyde does not tear it up in Ralph's presence, it is probably not effectively revoked.

REVIVAL   What if you change your will by drafting a new one, and later decide you do not like the changes and want to go back to your old will? You cannot destroy the new one and revive the old one. Once you execute a new will revoking an old will, you cannot revive the old will unless you execute a new document stating that you intend to revive the old will. In other words, you really should execute a new will.

CHANGING YOUR WILL

You should not make any changes to your will after it has been signed. If you cross out a person's name or add a clause to a will that has already been signed, your change will not be valid and your entire will might become invalid.

One way to amend a will is to execute a CODICIL. A CODICIL is an amendment to a will. However, a CODICIL must be executed just like a will. It must have the same number of witnesses, and to be self-proved it must include a self-proving page that must be notarized. (see form 20, p.109.)

Because a CODICIL requires the same formality as a will, it is usually better to make a new will. Also, if you are removing gifts to some of your children or relatives, you might wish to create a new will to prevent bad feelings.

In an emergency situation, if you want to change something in your will, but cannot get to a notary to have it self-proved, you can execute a CODICIL that is witnessed, but not self-proved. As long as the CODICIL is properly witnessed (by two witnesses), it will legally change your will. The only drawback is that the witnesses must later sign an oath.

HOW TO MAKE A LIVING WILL **6**

A *living will* is a document in which a person declares that he or she does not want artificial life support systems used if he or she becomes terminally ill. In Texas, this document is called a DIRECTIVE. It has nothing to do with the usual type of will that distributes property.

Modern science can often keep a body alive even if the brain is permanently dead or the person is in constant pain. All states have legalized living wills either by statute or by court decision.

A DIRECTIVE must be signed in front of two witnesses who should not be blood relatives or a spouse. If the person is physically unable to sign, he or she may read the DIRECTIVE out loud and direct one of the witnesses to sign it for him or her. A DIRECTIVE can be in the form included in the Texas statutes or it can be rewritten. But to be sure it will be valid, it is best to use the statutory form. (see form 21, p.111.)

HOW TO DESIGNATE A HEALTH CARE AGENT

7

There may be a time when a person is unable to make decisions regarding his or her routine medical care. This may occur when a person has been in an automobile accident, is unconscious and unable to talk with doctors about tests, x-rays, or even surgery that may be needed. In this situation, an individual designated by the patient as a "health care agent" can make such decisions until the patient regains the ability to make decisions regarding routine medical care.

In Texas, a MEDICAL POWER OF ATTORNEY AND DESIGNATION OF HEALTH CARE AGENT can be signed by a person in advance of such situations. Then, in the event the need arises, the health care agent can present the document to the doctors and make health care decisions. This form must be signed in front of two witnesses who should not be blood relatives, a spouse, or a medical professional. The statutory MEDICAL POWER OF ATTORNEY AND DESIGNATION OF HEALTH CARE AGENT form is included in Appendix C as form 22, p.115.

How to Designate a Guardian for Yourself

8

As our population lives longer, it has become increasingly common for a guardianship to be established for an older individual. This process requires the involvement of the court. The court may appoint a family member, friend, or an unrelated party to serve as a person's guardian. The person for whom the guardianship is being obtained (often called the *ward*) has no input into who will serve as his or her guardian. Among family members, it may be a "race to the courthouse" to see who will be appointed as guardian. The court would have to find compelling reasons not to appoint a particular family member as guardian. Mere allegations that the family member and the ward do not get along will not keep that family member from being appointed.

Texas law permits a person to designate someone to serve as his or her guardian in the event the person becomes incapacitated and must have a guardian. The statutory form is included in Appendix C as form 23, p.121.

How to Designate a Guardian and Health Care Agent for Children 9

Texas law contains two important documents that a person can sign relating to the welfare of his or her children.

The first document is the DECLARATION OF APPOINTMENT OF GUARDIAN FOR MY CHILDREN IN THE EVENT OF MY DEATH OR INCAPACITY. This statutory form is included in Appendix C as form 24.

If a parent dies with a will and has designated a guardian for his or her minor children, the guardian provisions in the will control. However, if a parent dies without a will or dies with a will that does not contain a guardianship designation but has signed a DECLARATION OF APPOINTMENT OF GUARDIAN, the court will give preference to such designation unless the court finds that it is not in the best interests of the children to be raised by the person designated.

If a parent becomes incapacitated, whether permanently or temporarily, it is very important that his or her wishes be known as to who will raise the minor children during the period of incapacity. Many times family members will argue about who will take care of the children and may have to go to court to have the differences settled. A DECLARATION OF APPOINTMENT OF GUARDIAN would avoid this family squabbling.

Example: Jane is a single parent, and is in a car accident and has suffered head injuries. She will require several months of hospitalization and rehabilitation. Her ex-husband lives in another state and is unable to take care of the children. Jane had signed a DECLARATION OF APPOINTMENT OF GUARDIAN naming her sister as guardian. Her sister would have all the legal rights of a guardian of the children until Jane recovers.

How to Make Anatomical Gifts 10

Texas residents are allowed to donate their bodies or organs for research or transplantation. Consent may be given by a relative of a deceased person, but because relatives are often in shock or too upset to make such a decision, it is better to have one's intent made clear before death. Consent can be given through a statement in a will or through another signed document such as a UNIFORM DONOR CARD. (see form 25, p.125.) Texas residents may also make such a statement on the back of their driver's license. The gift may be all or part of one's body. It may be made to a specific person, such as a physician or an ill relative.

The document making the donation must be signed before two witnesses, who must also sign in each other's presence. If the donor cannot sign, then the document may be signed for him or her at his or her direction in the presence of the witnesses. The donor may even designate in the document which physician will carry out the procedure.

If the document or will has been delivered to a specific donee, it may be amended or revoked by the donor through:

- the execution and delivery of a signed statement to the donee;

- an oral statement to two witnesses who tell the donee;

- an oral statement during a terminal illness made to an attending physician who tells the donee; or,

- a signed document found with the donor or in his or her effects.

If a document of donation has not been delivered to a donee, it may be revoked by any of the above methods or by destruction, cancellation, or mutilation of the document. It may also be revoked in the same method a will is revoked as described on page 32.

GLOSSARY

A

administrator (*administratrix* if female). A person appointed by the court to oversee distribution of the property of someone who died (either without a will, or if the person designated in the will is unable to serve).

alternate beneficiary. A person who is entitled to receive property from a person who died, only if the first beneficiary named is not alive or is not entitled to receive the property.

annual exclusion. The amount of property a person can give to another person per year which is not counted against the lifetime unified credit.

attested will. A will which includes an attestation clause and has been signed in front of witnesses and notary public.

B

beneficiary. A person who is entitled to receive property from a person who died (regardless of whether there is a will).

bequest. Personal property (including cash, stocks, etc.) left to someone in a will.

C

children's trust. A trust set up to hold property given to children. Usually it provides that the children will not receive their property until they reach a higher age than the age of majority.

codicil. An amendment to a will.

community property. Property acquired during marriage that was not a gift to or inheritance of one spouse or is specifically kept separate. This includes wages, income on investments, and income from business.

D

decedent. A person who has died.

declaration of guardian in advance of later incapacity or need of guardian. A document by which a person designates one or more persons to act as his or her guardian in the event the person becomes incapacitated.

dependent estate administration. Executor's actions and records are audited or approved by the probate court. Executor is required to obtain court's prior approval to pay debts, collects assets, pay taxes, or distribute assets to beneficiaries.

descendent. A child, grandchild, great-grandchild, etc.

devise. Real property left to someone in a will. A person who is entitled to a devise is called a *devisee*.

E

elective share. In non-community property states, the portion of the estate which may be taken by a surviving spouse, regardless of what the will says.

executor (*executrix* if female). A person appointed in a will to oversee distribution of the property of someone who died with a will.

estate tax. Type of death tax based on the decedent's right to transfer property; not a tax on the property itself.

exempt property. Property that is exempt from distribution as a normal part of the estate.

F

family allowance. An amount deemed reasonable by the court which is paid to the surviving spouse and children of the decedent to defray living expenses during the year following death.

federal estate tax. Federal tax assessed against the assets of a person who has died if the value of the taxable assets exceeds $1,000,000.

forced share. *See* **elective share**.

G

guardian of incompetent. Person or corporation appointed by a court to handle the affairs or property of another who is unable to do so because of incapacity.

guardian of minor child. Person or persons named to have custody of and raise minor children

H

handwritten will (Also known as a holographic will). All material provisions are entirely in the handwriting of the maker and the will is signed by the maker.

heir. A person who will inherit from a decedent who died without a will.

holographic will. A will in which all of the material provisions are entirely in the handwriting of the maker. Holographic wills are legal in Texas.

homestead. A person's principal place of residence as designated with the county recorder.

I

incapacitated/incompetent. One who is unable to manage his or her own affairs either temporarily or permanently.

independent estate administration. Executor's actions and records are not audited or approved by the probate court. Executor is not required to obtain court's prior approval to pay debts, collects assets, pay taxes, or distribute assets to beneficiaries.

inheritance tax. Tax imposed on property received by beneficiaries from the estate of a decedent.

intestate. Without making a will. One who dies without a will is said to have *died intestate.*

intestate share. In non-community property states, the portion of the estate a spouse is entitled to receive if there is no will.

J

joint tenancy. A type of property ownership by two or more persons, in which if one owner dies, that owner's interest goes to the other joint tenants (not to the deceased owner's heirs as in tenancy in common).

joint tenancy with right of survivorship (JTWROS). Form of ownership in which property is equally shared by all owners and is automatically transferred to the surviving owners when one of them dies.

L

legacy. Real property left to someone in a will. A person who is entitled to a legacy is called a *legatee*.

living (or inter vivos) trust. A revocable trust separate from a will which may be funded or unfunded during the settlor's lifetime. It is commonly used to avoid probate and provide a means for the management of assets during incompetency or incapacity.

living will. A document expressing the writer's desires regarding how medical care is to be handled in the event the writer is not able to express his or her wishes concerning the use of life-prolonging medical procedures.

M

medical power of attorney. A document that designates one or more persons to make routine health care decisions in the event a person is unable to give informed consent and make such decisions himself.

P

payable on death account (POD). An account that is automatically paid to a beneficiary named by the owner of the account upon the death of the account owner. The beneficiary has no rights to the account during his or her lifetime.

per capita. Distribution of property with equal shares going to each person.

per stirpes. Distribution of property with equal shares going to each family line.

personal property. Property that is movable, not land or things attached to land.

personal property memorandum. A document separate from the will that designates distribution of personal effects. This document is not legally effective but evidences a person's intent regarding distribution of personal effects.

personal representative. A person appointed by the court, or will, to oversee distribution of the property of the person who died. This is a more modern term than "administrator," "executor," etc., and applies regardless of whether there is a will.

power of attorney. Legal document whereby one person authorizes another to make medical and financial decisions should illness or incapacitation occur.

probate. Legal process of establishing the validity of a deceased person's last will and testament; commonly refers to the process and laws for settling an estate.

R

real property. Property that's immovable, such as land, buildings and whatever else is attached to or growing on land.

residue. The property that is left over in an estate after all specific bequests and devises.

S

self-proving affidavit. A form added to a will in which the will maker and witnesses state under oath in front of a notary public that they have signed and witnessed the will.

separate property. Property owned by a spouse prior to marriage or acquired by the spouse during marriage by gift, inheritance or as a result of a personal injury settlement.

specific bequest *or* **specific devise**. A gift in a will of a specific item of property, or a specific amount of cash.

statutory will. A will which has been prepared according to the requirements of a statute.

T

tenancy by entirety. Form of spousal ownership in which property is equally shared and automatically transferred to the surviving spouse. While both spouses are living, ownership of the property can be altered only by divorce or mutual agreement.

tenancy in common. Ownership of property by two or more people, in which each owner's share would descend to that owner's heirs (not to the other owners as in joint tenancy).

testamentary trust. Trust established in a person's will.

testate. With a will. One who dies with a will is said to have *died testate*.

testator (*testatrix* if female). A person who makes his or her will.

Totten trust. Revocable trust created by the owner of a bank account (checking, savings or other) for the future benefit of another.

trust. Real or personal property held by one party (the trustee) for the benefit of another (the beneficiary).

trustee. Person who holds and/or manages money or property for the benefit of another.

U

unified credit. The federal credit against estate taxes which is allowed to each person or estate.

W

will. Legal document that declares how a person wishes property to be distributed to heirs or beneficiaries after death. It can only be enforced thru a probate court.

Appendix A

Explanation of Federal Estate Taxes Including Federal Estate and Gift Schedule

As discussed throughout the text, all property owned by you at your death (probate and non-probate), is subject to the federal estate tax at your death. The federal estate tax applies to all estates. However, the law grants you a *unified credit* and your estate does not have to pay tax on an amount up to that credit. In 2002, the unified credit is $1,000,000.

In June, 2001, President Bush signed a new tax law which contains among its provisions, drastic changes to the estate and gift tax law. Under the new law, the estate tax will be completely repealed by the year 2010. The new law also reduces the highest estate and gift tax rates. The following table sets forth the increase in the *unified credit* and the decrease in the estate and gift tax rate.

Calendar Year	Estate and Gift Tax Unified Credit Amount	Highest Estate & Gift Tax Rate
2002	$1 million	50%
2003	$1 million	49%
2004	$1.5 million	48%
2005	$1.5 million	47%
2006	$2 million	46%
2007	$2 million	45%
2008	$2 million	45%
2009	$3.5 million	45%
2010	N/A	Replaced by top individual income tax rate (gifts only)

The gift tax is not repealed. Instead, there is a new $1 million lifetime exemption for gifts beginning in 2002. In 2010, the maximum gift tax rate on gifts in excess of $1 million will be 35%.

Under the current law, when an individual inherits property and later sells it, the person does not have to pay capital gains tax on the appreciation that occurred prior to the death of the person from whom they inherited the property. The heir is able to "step up" the basis of the asset to the value at the date of the decedent's death. Capital gain is then calculated from the date of death until the date of sale.

In 2010, however, with the repeal of the estate tax, the "step-up" in rules will change for property inherited from a decedent. A decedent's estate will be permitted to increase the basis of assets transferred to heirs up to a total of $1.3 million. The basis of property transferred to a surviving spouse could be increased by $3.0 million. Thus, the basis of property transferred to a surviving spouse could be increased by a total of $4.3 million.

For anyone who has an estate in excess of $1.3 million, there will still be a tax that will eventually be paid—a capital gains tax—by the beneficiary. The problems will come when executors, trustees, beneficiaries and their accountants have to determine the decedent's basis in assets to make the proper "step-up." There will also be problems later when a beneficiary sells assets that did not receive a step-up in basis upon the decedent's death.

NOTE: *The new law provides that there will be no estate tax in the year 2010. It also provides that unless Congress takes action before December 31, 2010, the estate tax will come back into effect. Then, the unified credit exemption will only be $1,000,000 for each decedent.*

APPENDIX B
SAMPLE FILLED-IN FORMS

The following pages include sample filled-in forms for *some* of the wills in this book. They are filled out in different ways for different situations. You should look at all of them to see how the different sections can be filled in. Only one example of a self-proved will affidavit is shown, but you should use it with every will.

Last Will and Testament

I, _____John Doe_____ a resident of __Leon__ County, Texas do hereby make, publish and declare this to be my Last Will and Testament, hereby revoking any and all Wills and Codicils heretofore made by me.

FIRST: I direct that all my just debts and funeral expenses be paid out of my estate as soon after my death as is practicable.

SECOND: I give and bequeath the following personal property unto the following persons:

My gold pocketwatch	to	James Doe
My antique bookcase	to	Sally Doe
--------------------	to	--------------------

THIRD: All the rest, residue and remainder of my estate, real or personal, whereso-ever situate, now owned or hereafter acquired by me, which at the time of my death shall belong to me or be subject to my disposal by will, I give, devise and bequeath unto my spouse, ____Mary Doe____. If my said spouse does not survive me, I give, and bequeath the said property to my children ____James Doe, Mary Doe, Larry Doe, Barry Doe, Carrie Doe, and Moe Doe____ plus any afterborn or adopted children in equal shares.

FOURTH: In the event that any beneficiary fails to survive me by thirty days, then this will shall take effect as if that person had predeceased me.

FIFTH: Should my spouse not survive me, I hereby nominate, constitute and appoint ____Mary Doe____, as guardian over the person of any of my children who have not reached the age of majority at the time of my death. In the event that said guardian is unable or unwilling to serve then I nominate, constitute and appoint ____Madeleine Doe____ as guardian. Said guardian to serve without bond or surety.

SIXTH: Should my spouse not survive me, I hereby nominate, constitute and appoint ____Mary Doe____ as guardian over the estate of any of my children who have not reached the age of majority at the time of my death. In the event that said guardian is unable or unwilling to serve then I nominate, constitute and appoint ____Englebert Doe____ as guardian. Said guardian to serve without bond or surety.

SEVENTH: I hereby nominate, constitute and appoint ____Mary Doe____ to serve as Executor of this, my Last Will and Testament, to serve without bond or surety. In the event that he or she is unable or unwilling to serve at any time or for any reason then I nominate, constitute and appoint ____Englebert Doe____ as alternate Executor also to serve without bond or surety. I give my said Executor the fullest power in all matters including the power to sell or convey real or personal property or any interest therein with-out court order. My Executor shall serve as an independent executor, and no action shall be

Page _1_ of ____

had in the county court in relation to the settlement of my estate other than the probating and recording of my Will and the return of an inventory, appraisement and list of claims of my estate, as provided by law.

IN WITNESS WHEREOF I declare this to be my Last Will and Testament and execute it willingly as my free and voluntary act for the purposes expressed herein and I am of legal age and sound mind and make this under no constraint or undue influence, this <u>5th</u> day of <u>January</u>, <u>2003</u>.

<u>*John Doe*</u> L.S.

The foregoing instrument was on said date subscribed at the end thereof by <u>John Doe</u>, the above named Testator who signed, published, and declared this instrument to be his/her Last Will and Testament in the presence of us and each of us, who thereupon at his/her request, in his/her presence, and in the presence of each other, have hereunto subscribed our names as witnesses thereto. We understand this to be his/her will and to the best of our knowledge testator is of legal age, of sound mind and under no constraint or undue influence.

<u>*Rick Richards*</u> residing at <u>*5432 South Street*</u>

<u>*Robert Robinson*</u> residing at <u>*1234 Main Street*</u>

Last Will and Testament

I, <u>John Smith</u> a resident of <u>Hockley</u> County, Texas do hereby make, publish and declare this to be my Last Will and Testament, hereby revoking any and all Wills and Codicils heretofore made by me.

FIRST: I direct that all my just debts and funeral expenses be paid out of my estate as soon after my death as is practicable.

SECOND: I give and bequeath the following personal property unto the following persons:

My gold pocketwatch	to	Danny Smith
My antique bookcase	to	Sally Smith
--------------------	to	--------------------

THIRD: All the rest, residue and remainder of my estate, real or personal, whereso-ever situate, now owned or hereafter acquired by me, which at the time of my death shall belong to me or be subject to my disposal by will, I give, devise and bequeath unto my spouse, <u>Barbara Smith</u>. If my said spouse does not survive me, I give, and bequeath the said property to my children <u>Amy Smith, Beamy Smith and Seamy Smith in equal shares</u>, in equal shares or to their lineal descendants, per stirpes.

FOURTH: In the event that any beneficiary fails to survive me by thirty days, then this will shall take effect as if that person had predeceased me.

FIFTH: I hereby nominate, constitute and appoint <u>Barbara Smith</u> to serve as Executor of this, my Last Will and Testament, to serve without bond or surety. In the event that he or she is unable or unwilling to serve at any time or for any reason then I nominate, constitute and appoint <u>Reginald Smith</u> as alternate Executor also to serve without bond or surety. I give my said Executor the fullest power in all matters including the power to sell or convey real or personal property or any interest therein without court order. My Executor shall serve as an independent executor, and no action shall be had in the county court in relation to the settlement of my estate other than the probating and recording of my Will and the return of an inventory, appraisement and list of claims of my estate, as provided by law.

IN WITNESS WHEREOF I declare this to be my Last Will and Testament and execute it willingly as my free and voluntary act for the purposes expressed herein and I am of legal age and sound mind and make this under no constraint or undue influence, this <u>5th</u> day of <u>January</u>, <u>2003</u>.

John Smith

Page <u>1</u> of <u> </u>

Last Will and Testament

I, _____John Doe_____ a resident of ____Leon____ County, Texas do hereby make, publish and declare this to be my Last Will and Testament, hereby revoking any and all Wills and Codicils heretofore made by me.

FIRST: I direct that all my just debts and funeral expenses be paid out of my estate as soon after my death as is practicable.

SECOND: I give and bequeath the following personal property unto the following persons:

____My gold pocketwatch____ to ____James Doe____

____My antique bookcase____ to ____Sally Doe____

____-------------------____ to ____-------------------____

THIRD: All the rest, residue and remainder of my estate, real or personal, whereso-ever situate, now owned or hereafter acquired by me, which at the time of my death shall belong to me or be subject to my disposal by will, I give, devise and bequeath unto my children ____James Doe, Mary Doe, Larry Doe, Barry Doe, Carrie Doe, and Moe Doe____ _____ _____, plus any afterborn or adopted children in equal shares or to their lineal descendants per stir-pes.

FOURTH: In the event that any beneficiary fails to survive me by thirty days, then this will shall take effect as if that person had predeceased me.

FIFTH: In the event that any of my children have not reached the age of ____25____ years at the time of my death, then the share of any such child shall be held IN TRUST by ____James Doe____ until such time as such child or children reach the age of ____25____ years. The trustee shall use the income and that part of the principal of the trust as is, in the discretion of the trustee, necessary or desirable to provide proper housing, medical care, food, clothing, entertainment and education for the trust beneficiaries. In the event the said trustee is unable or unwilling to serve for any reason, then I nominate, consti-tute and appoint ____Sally Doe____ as alternate trustee. No bond shall be required of either trustee in any jurisdiction.

SIXTH: In the event any of my children have not attained the age of 18 years at the time of my death, I hereby nominate, constitute and appoint ____Sally Doe____ _____ as guardian over the property of any of my children who have not reached the age of majority at the time of my death. In the event that said guardian is unable or unwilling to serve then I nominate, constitute and appoint ____Madeleine Small____ _____ as guardian. Said guardian to serve without bond or surety.

SEVENTH: I hereby nominate, constitute and appoint ____James Doe____ to serve as Executor of this, my Last Will and Testament, to serve without bond or surety. In

Page ____1____ of ____

57

the event that he or she is unable or unwilling to serve at any time or for any reason then I nominate, constitute and appoint ___Englebert Doe_____ as alternate Executor also to serve without bond or surety. I give my said Executor the fullest power in all matters including the power to sell or convey real or personal property or any interest therein without court order. My Executor shall serve as an independent executor, and no action shall be had in the county court in relation to the settlement of my estate other than the probating and recording of my Will and the return of an inventory, appraisement and list of claims of my estate, as provided by law.

IN WITNESS WHEREOF I declare this to be my Last Will and Testament and execute it willingly as my free and voluntary act for the purposes expressed herein and I am of legal age and sound mind and make this under no constraint or undue influence, this 5th day of __January_____, _2003_.

*John Doe*_____

The foregoing instrument was on said date subscribed at the end thereof by _____John Doe_____, the above named Testator who signed, published, and declared this instrument to be his/her Last Will and Testament in the presence of us and each of us, who thereupon at his/her request, in his/her presence, and in the presence of each other, have hereunto subscribed our names as witnesses thereto. We understand this to be his/her will and to the best of our knowledge testator is of legal age, of sound mind and under no constraint or undue influence.

___*Rick Richards*_____residing at_*5432 South Street*_____

___*Robert Robinson*_____residing at_*1234 Main Street*_____

Last Will and Testament

I, <u>John Smith</u> a resident of <u>Hockley</u> County, Texas do hereby make, publish and declare this to be my Last Will and Testament, hereby revoking any and all Wills and Codicils heretofore made by me.

FIRST: I direct that all my just debts and funeral expenses be paid out of my estate as soon after my death as is practicable.

SECOND: I give and bequeath the following personal property unto the following persons:

My gold pocketwatch	to	Danny Smith
My antique bookcase	to	Sally Smith
--------------------	to	--------------------

THIRD: All the rest, residue and remainder of my estate, real or personal, wheresoever situate, now owned or hereafter acquired by me, which at the time of my death shall belong to me or be subject to my disposal by will, I give, devise and bequeath unto the following 75% to my dear friend, Frannie Farkle, or her lineal descendants, per stirpes; 15% to the Hockley County Humane Soc.; 10% to Texas Tech. University----- --, ~~in equal shares, or their lineal descendants per stirpes.~~

FOURTH: In the event that any beneficiary fails to survive me by thirty days, then this will shall take effect as if that person had predeceased me.

FIFTH: I hereby nominate, constitute and appoint <u>Frannie Farkle</u> to serve as Executor of this, my Last Will and Testament, to serve without bond or surety. In the event that he or she is unable or unwilling to serve at any time or for any reason then I nominate, constitute and appoint <u>Danny Smith</u> as alternate Executor also to serve without bond or surety. I give my said Executor the fullest power in all matters including the power to sell or convey real or personal property or any interest therein without court order. My Executor shall serve as an independent executor, and no action shall be had in the county court in relation to the settlement of my estate other than the probating and recording of my Will and the return of an inventory, appraisement and list of claims of my estate, as provided by law.

IN WITNESS WHEREOF I declare this to be my Last Will and Testament and execute it willingly as my free and voluntary act for the purposes expressed herein and I am of legal age and sound mind and make this under no constraint or undue influence, this <u>29th</u> day of <u>January</u>, <u>2003</u>.

<u>*John Smith*</u>

Page <u>1</u> of <u>   </u>

Self-Proving Affidavit

STATE OF TEXAS   §
                                                     §
COUNTY OF ____Eldorado____   §

      BEFORE ME, the undersigned authority, on this day personally appeared
_____John Doe_____, _____Melvin Coe_____
and_____Jane Roe_____, known to me to be the Testator and the witnesses, respectively, whose names are subscribed to the annexed or foregoing instrument in their respective capacities; and all of said persons being by me duly sworn, the Testator declared to me and to the witnesses in my presence that said instrument is his/her Will, and that he/she had willingly made and executed it as his/her free act and deed for the purposes therein expressed; and the witnesses, each on his oath, stated to me in the presence and hearing of the Testator that the Testator had declared to them that said instrument is his/her Will, and that he/she executed same as such and wanted each of them to sign it as a witness; and upon their oaths each witness stated further that they did sign the same as witnesses in the presence of the Testator and at his/her request, that he/she was at that time eighteen (18) years of age or over and was of sound mind, and that each of the witnesses was then at least fourteen (14) years of age.

_____*John Doe*_____
TESTATOR

_____*Jane Roe*_____
WITNESS

_____*Melvin Coe*_____
WITNESS

SUBSCRIBED AND ACKNOWLEDGED before me by ____John Doe_____, the Testator and subscribed and sworn to before me by the above-named witnesses this _____5th_____ day of _____July____, __2003__ .

_____*C.U. Sine*_____
Notary Public

Page 1____ of ____

First Codicil to the Will of

<u>Larry Lowe</u>

I, <u>Larry Lowe</u>, a resident of <u>Eldorado</u> County, Texas declare this to be the first codicil to my Last Will and Testament dated <u>July 5</u>, <u>1999</u>.

FIRST: I hereby revoke the clause of my Will which reads as follows: _____
<u>FOURTH: I hereby leave $5000.00 to my daughter Mildred Lowe</u>
_____
_____

SECOND: I hereby add following clause to my Will: _____
<u>FOURTH: I hereby leave $1000.00 to my daughter Mildred Lowe</u>
_____
_____

THIRD: In all other respects I hereby confirm and republish my Last Will and Testament dated <u>July 5</u>, <u>1999</u>.

Date: <u>January 15, 2000</u>   *Larry Lowe*

We, the undersigned persons, of lawful age, have on this <u>5th</u> day of <u>July</u>, <u>1999</u>, at the request of <u>Larry Lowe</u>, witnessed his/her signature to the foregoing First Codicil to Will in the presence of each of us; and we have, at the same time and in his/her presence and in the presence of each other, subscribed our names hereto as attesting witnesses.

Michael Smith   residing at: <u>21 Oak Lane</u>
_____   <u>Ft. Worth, TX 76011</u>

Mary Smith   residing at: <u>121 Wall St.</u>
_____   <u>Ft. Worth, TX 76102</u>

SELF-PROVING AFFIDAVIT

STATE OF TEXAS   §
                             §
COUNTY OF <u>Eldorado</u>   §

BEFORE ME, the undersigned authority, on this day personally appeared <u>Larry Lowe</u> _____, <u>Michael Smith</u>, and <u>Mary Smith</u>, known to me to be the Testator and the witnesses, respectively, whose names are subscribed to the annexed or foregoing instrument in their respective capacities; and all of said persons being by me duly sworn, the Testator declared to me and to the witnesses in my presence that said instrument is his/her First Codicil to Will, and that he/she had willingly made and executed it as his/her free act and deed for the purposes therein expressed; and the witnesses, each on his oath, stated to me in the presence and hearing of the Testator that the Testator had declared to them that said instrument is his/her First Codicil to Will, and that he/she executed same as such and wanted each of them to sign it as a witness; and upon their oaths each witness stated further that they did sign the same as witnesses in the presence of the Testator and at his/her request, that he/she was at that time eighteen (18) years of age or over and was of sound mind, and that each of the witnesses was then at least fourteen (14) years of age.

Larry Lowe   *Michael Smith*
_____   _____
TESTATOR   WITNESS
                                      Mary Smith
                                      _____
                                      WITNESS

SUBSCRIBED AND ACKNOWLEDGED before me by <u>Larry Lowe</u>, the Testator and subscribed and sworn to before me by the above-named witnesses this <u>5th</u> day of <u>July</u>, <u>1999</u>.

Arthur Izer
_____
Notary Public   Page <u>1</u> of ____

DIRECTIVE

I, _____John Doe_____, recognize that the best health care is based upon a partnership of trust and communication with my physician. My physician and I will make health care decisions together as long as I am of sound mind and able to make my wishes known. If there comes a time that I am unable to make medical decisions about myself because of illness or injury, I direct that the following treatment preferences be honored:

If, in the judgment of my physician, I am suffering with a terminal condition from which I am expected to die within six months, even with available life-sustaining treatment provided in accordance with prevailing standards of medical care:

___JD___ I request that all treatments other than those needed to keep me comfortable be discontinued or withheld and my physician allow me to die as gently as possible; OR

_____ I request that I be kept alive in this terminal condition using available life-sustaining treatment. (THIS SELECTION DOES NOT APPLY TO HOSPICE CARE.)

If, in the judgment of my physician, I am suffering with an irreversible condition so that I cannot care for myself or make decisions for myself and am expected to die without life-sustaining treatment provided in accordance with prevailing standards of medical care:

___JD___ I request that all treatment other than those needed to keep me comfortable be discontinued or withheld and my physician allow me to die as gently as possible; OR

_____ I request that I be kept alive in this irreversible condition using available life-sustaining treatment. (THIS SELECTION DOES NOT APPLY TO HOSPICE CARE.)

Additional requests: (After discussion with your physician, you may wish to consider listing particular treatments in this space that you do or do not want in specific circumstances, such as artificial nutrition and fluids, intravenous antibiotics, etc. Be sure to state whether you do or do not want the particular treatment.)

_____

_____

After signing this directive, if my representative or I elect hospice care, I understand and agree that only those treatments needed to keep me comfortable would be provided and I would not be given available life-sustaining treatments.

If I do not have a Medical Power of Attorney, and I am unable to make my wishes known, I designate the following person(s) to make treatment decisions with my physician compatible with my personal values:

Page 1 of ____

1. _____
2. _____

(If a Medical Power of Attorney has been executed, than an agent already has been named and you should not list additional names in this document.)

If the above persons are not available, or if I have not designated a spokesperson, I understand that a spokesperson will be chosen for me following standards specified in the laws of Texas. If, in the judgment of my physician, my death is imminent within minutes to hours, even with the use of all available medical treatment provided within the prevailing standard of care, I acknowledge that all treatments may be withheld or removed except those needed to maintain my comfort. I understand that under Texas law this directive has no effect if I have been diagnosed as pregnant. This directive will remain in effect until I revoke it. No other person may do so.

Signed this __12th__ day of ___October___ , __2003__ , in __San Antonio,__ __Bexar_____ County, Texas.

_____*John Doe*_____
[Print Name]: __John Doe_____

The witnesses acknowledge that the declarant signed this directive in their presence and that each of them is over the age of eighteen (18) years and competent to witness this document. The witness designated at "Witness 1" is: (1) not a person designated by the declarant to make a treatment decision for the declarant; (2) not related to the declarant by blood or marriage; (3) not entitled to any portion of the declarant's estate on declarant's death; (4) not a claimant against the estate of the declarant; (5) not the attending physician or employee of the attending physician of declarant; and (6) not an officer, director, partner, or business office employee of a health care facility in which the declarant is being cared for or of any parent organization of the health care facility. Furthermore, if "Witness 1" is an employee of a health care facility in which the declarant is a patient, such witness is not involved in providing direct patient care to the declarant.

_____*Richard Anderson*_____
Witness 1
Address:__35 Cedar Street__
_____San Antonio, Texas__

_____*Sally Jones*_____
Witness 2
Address:__123 Main Street__
_____San Antonio, Texas__

Page 2 of ____

MEDICAL POWER OF ATTORNEY
AND DESIGNATION OF HEALTH CARE AGENT

1. DESIGNATION OF HEALTH CARE AGENT

I, _____ Mary Smith _____, appoint:

Name: Michael Smith
Address: 55 Elm Avenue
              Houston, Texas
Phone: (713) 333-1211

as my agent to make any and all health care decisions for me, except to the extent I state otherwise in this document. This Medical Power of Attorney takes effect if I become unable to make my own health care decisions and this fact is certified in writing by my physician.

LIMITATIONS ON THE DECISION MAKING AUTHORITY OF MY AGENT ARE AS FOLLOWS:
_____ NONE _____

_____

2. DESIGNATION OF ALTERNATE AGENT

(You are not required to designate an alternate agent but you may do so. An alternate agent may make the same health care decisions as the designated agent if the designated agent is unable or unwilling to act as your agent. If the agent designated is your spouse, the designation is automatically revoked by law if your marriage is dissolved).

If the person designated as my agent is unable or unwilling to make health care decisions for me, I designate the following person to serve as my agent to make health care decisions for me as authorized by this document:

First Alternate Agent

Name: Susan Johnson
Address: 1367 Riverside Way
              Dallas, Texas
Phone: (214) 498-5601

Page 1___ of ____

<u>Second Alternate Agent</u>

Name: <u>NOT APPLICABLE</u>
Address: <u>   </u>

                      <u>   </u>

Phone: <u>   </u>

An original of this document is kept at:

> <u>666 Holley Lane</u>
> <u>San Antonio, Texas</u>

The following individuals or institutions have signed copies:

Name: <u>Michael Smith</u>
Address: <u>55 Elm Avenue</u>

                      <u>Houston, Texas</u>

Phone: <u>(713) 333-1211</u>

Name: <u>Susan Johnson</u>
Address: <u>1367 Riverside Way</u>

                      <u>Dallas, Texas</u>

Phone: <u>(214) 498-5601</u>

3.   <u>DURATION</u>

I understand that this Medical Power of Attorney exists indefinitely from the date I execute this document unless I establish a shorter time or revoke the power of attorney. If I am unable to make health care decisions for myself when this power of attorney expires, the authority I have granted my agent continues to exist until the time I become able to make health care decisions for myself.

(IF APPLICABLE) This Medical Power of Attorney ends on the following date:

_____

4.   <u>PRIOR DESIGNATIONS REVOKED</u>

I revoke any prior Medical Power of Attorney.

5.   <u>ACKNOWLEDGMENT OF DISCLOSURE STATEMENT</u>

I have been provided with a disclosure statement explaining the effect of this document. I have read and understand that information contained in the disclosure statement.

(YOU MUST DATE AND SIGN THIS POWER OF ATTORNEY.)

I sign my name to this Medical Power of Attorney on the <u> 12th </u> day of <u> October,</u> 20 <u>03 </u>, at <u> San Antonio </u>, <u> Bexar </u> County, Texas.

<u> *Mary Smith* </u>
Print Name: <u>Mary Smith</u>

STATEMENT AND SIGNATURE OF FIRST WITNESS:

I am not the person appointed as agent by this document. I am not related to the principal by blood or marriage. I would not be entitled to any portion of the principal¢s estate on the principal¢s death. I am not the attending physician of the principal or an employee of the attending physician. I have no claim against any portion of the principal¢s estate on the principal¢s death. Furthermore, if I am an employee of a health care facility in which the principal is a patient, I am not involved in providing direct patient care to the principal and am not an officer, director, partner, or business office employee of the health care facility or of any parent organization of the health care facility.

Witness Signature: <u> *Sally Jones* </u>
Print Name: <u>Sally Jones </u>   Date: <u>October 12, 2003</u>
Address: <u>   123 Main Street, San Antonio, Texas </u>

SIGNATURE OF SECOND WITNESS:

Witness Signature: <u> *Richard Anderson* </u>
Print Name: <u>Richard Anderson </u>   Date: <u>October 12, 2003</u>
Address: <u>   35 Cedar Street, San Antonio, Texas </u>

APPENDIX C
FORMS

The following pages contain forms which can be used to prepare a will, codicil, directive to physicians, and organ donor card. They should only be used by persons who have read this book, who do not have any complications in their legal affairs and who understand the forms they are using. The forms may be used right out of the book or they may be photocopied or retyped.

This will should be used if you wish to leave your property to your adult children, or equally to each **family** *if they predecease you.*

This will should be used if you wish to leave your property to your adult children, or equally to each **person** *if they predecease you.*

Use this will if you have no spouse or children and want your property to go to the **survivor** *of the people you name.*

Use this will if you have no spouse or children and want your property to go to the **children and grandchildren** *of the people you name.*

This affidavit should be executed by you and the witnesses to your will at the time of executing your will.

This form can be used to change one section of your will. Usually it is just as easy to execute a new will, since all of the same formalities are required.

This is a document which expresses your desire to withhold certain extraordinary medical treatment should you have a terminal illness and you reach such a state that your wishes to withhold such treatment cannot be determined.

This form is used to spell out your wishes for donation of your body or any organs and can be carried in your wallet or purse.

How to Pick the Right Will

Follow the chart and use the form number in the black circle—
then use form 19, the self -proving affidavit.

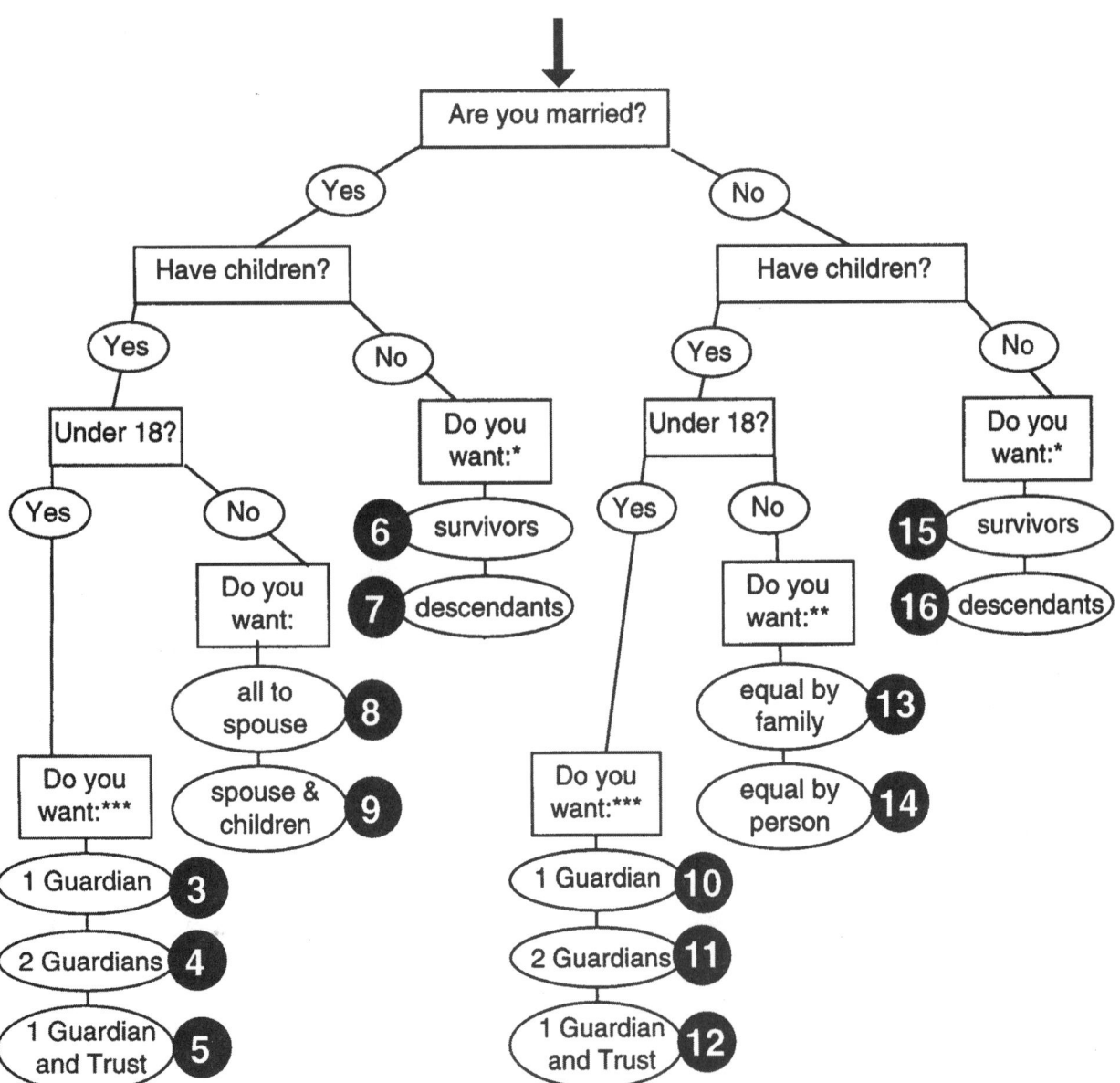

17 Be sure to use form 19, the self-proving affidavit with your will, no matter which fomr you use.

* For an explanation of survivors/descendants see page 24.

** For an explanation of families/persons see page 23.

*** For an explanation of childrens' guardians and trust, see pages 24 and 25.

Asset and Beneficiary List

Property Inventory

Assets

Bank Accounts (checking, savings, certificates of deposit)

_____
_____
_____
_____
_____
_____
_____
_____

Real Estate

_____
_____
_____
_____
_____
_____
_____
_____

Vehicles (cars, trucks, boats, planes, RVs, etc.)

_____
_____
_____
_____
_____
_____
_____
_____

Personal Property (collections, jewelry, tools, artwork, household items, etc.)

_____
_____
_____
_____
_____
_____
_____
_____

_____

_____

_____

_____

_____

_____

_____

Stocks/Bonds/Mutual Funds

_____

_____

_____

_____

_____

_____

_____

_____

_____

_____

_____

Retirement Accounts (IRAs, 401(k)s, pension plans, etc.)

_____

_____

_____

_____

_____

_____

Receivables (mortgages held, notes, accounts receivable, personal loans)

_____

_____

_____

_____

_____

Life insurance

_____
_____
_____
_____
_____
_____
_____

Other property (trusts, partnerships, businesses, profit sharing, copyrights, etc.)

_____
_____
_____
_____
_____
_____
_____
_____

Liabilities

Real Estate Loans

_____
_____
_____
_____
_____
_____
_____

Vehicle Loans

_____
_____
_____
_____
_____
_____
_____

Other Secured Loans

_____
_____
_____
_____
_____
_____
_____
_____

Unsecured Loans and Debts (taxes, child support, judgments, etc.)

_____
_____
_____
_____
_____
_____
_____
_____

Beneficiary List

Name_____ Address_____ Phone_____

_____
_____
_____
_____
_____
_____
_____
_____

Preferences List

STATEMENT OF DESIRES AND LOCATION OF PROPERTY & DOCUMENTS

I, _____, am signing this document as the expression of my desires as to the matters stated below, and to inform my family members or other significant persons of the location of certain property and documents in the event of any emergency or of my death.

1. **Funeral Desires.** It is my desire that the following arrangements be made for my funeral and disposition of remains in the event of my death (state if you have made any arrangements, such as pre-paid burial plans, cemetery plots owned, etc.):

    ❏   Burial at _____
        _____.

    ❏   Cremation at _____
        _____.

    ❏   Other specific desires: _____
        _____
        _____.

2. **Pets.** I have the following pet(s): _____.
    The following are my desires concerning the care of said pet(s): _____
    _____
    _____.

3. **Notification.** I would like the following person(s) notified in the event of emergency or death (give name, address and phone number):

    _____
    _____
    _____
    _____
    _____

4. **Location of Documents.** The following is a list of important documents, and their location:

    ❏   Last Will and Testament, dated _____. Location: _____
        _____.

    ❏   Durable Power of Attorney, dated _____. Location: _____
        _____.

    ❏   Living Will, dated _____. Location: _____
        _____.

    ❏   Deed(s) to real estate (describe property location and location of deed):
        _____
        _____
        _____

    ❏   Title(s) to vehicles (cars, boats, etc.) (Describe vehicle, its location, and location of title, registration, or other documents):

_____
_____
_____
_____

❏ Life insurance policies (list name address & phone number of insurance company and insurance agent, policy number, and location of policy):

_____
_____
_____

❏ Other insurance policies (list type, company & agent, policy number, and location of policy):

_____
_____
_____

❏ Other: (list other documents such as stock certificates, bonds, certificates of deposit, etc., and their location):

_____
_____
_____

5.   **Location of Assets.** In addition to items readily visible in my home or listed above, I have the following assets:

❏ Safe deposit box located at _____, box number _____. Key located at: _____.

❏ Bank accounts (list name & address of bank, type of account, and account number):

_____

❏ Other (describe the item and give its location):

_____
_____
_____
_____
_____

6.   Other desires or information (state any desires or provide any information not given above; use additional sheets of paper if necessary):

_____
_____
_____
_____
_____

Dated: _____

_____
                              Signature

IMPORTANT ADVISORS

_____PHONE: _____
DOCTOR

_____PHONE: _____
CLERGYMAN

_____PHONE: _____
EMPLOYER

_____PHONE: _____
BUSINESS PARTNER

_____PHONE: _____
ATTORNEY

_____PHONE: _____
ACCOUNTANT

_____PHONE: _____
BANKER

_____PHONE: _____
GENERAL INSURANCE AGENT

_____PHONE: _____
LIFE INSURANCE AGENT

_____PHONE: _____
FINANCIAL ADVISOR

_____PHONE: _____
STOCKBROKER

_____PHONE: _____
LANDLORD/MORTGAGE HOLDER

_____PHONE: _____
OTHER

_____PHONE: _____
OTHER

EMERGENCY INFORMATION

NAME: _____DATE OF BIRTH: _____

SOCIAL SECURITY NUMBER: _____

SPOUSE: _____

ADDRESS: _____

TELEPHONE: _____

DATE OF MARRIAGE: _____

EMPLOYER: _____

EMPLOYER'S ADDRESS: _____

CHILDREN:

NAME: _____DATE OF BIRTH: _____

ADDRESS: _____

NAME: _____DATE OF BIRTH: _____

ADDRESS: _____

NAME: _____DATE OF BIRTH: _____

ADDRESS: _____

NAME: _____DATE OF BIRTH: _____

ADDRESS: _____

NAME: _____DATE OF BIRTH: _____

ADDRESS: _____

RELATIVES & FRIENDS:

NAME:_____

ADDRESS: _____

NAME:_____

ADDRESS: _____

NAME:_____

ADDRESS: _____

NAME:_____

ADDRESS: _____

NAME:_____

ADDRESS: _____

Last Will and Testament

I, _____ a resident of _____ County, Texas do hereby make, publish and declare this to be my Last Will and Testament, hereby revoking any and all Wills and Codicils heretofore made by me.

FIRST: I direct that all my just debts and funeral expenses be paid out of my estate as soon after my death as is practicable.

SECOND: I give and bequeath the following personal property unto the following persons:

_____ to _____
_____ to _____
_____ to _____

THIRD: All the rest, residue and remainder of my estate, real or personal, wheresoever situate, now owned or hereafter acquired by me, which at the time of my death shall belong to me or be subject to my disposal by will, I give, devise and bequeath unto my spouse, _____. If my said spouse does not survive me, I give, and bequeath the said property to my children _____
_____
_____,
plus any afterborn or adopted children in equal shares.

FOURTH: In the event that any beneficiary fails to survive me by thirty days, then this will shall take effect as if that person had predeceased me.

FIFTH: Should my spouse not survive me, I hereby nominate, constitute and appoint _____ as guardian over the person and estate of any of my children who have not reached the age of majority at the time of my death. In the event that said guardian is unable or unwilling to serve then I nominate, constitute and appoint _____ as guardian. Said guardian to serve without bond or surety.

SIXTH: I hereby nominate, constitute and appoint _____ to serve as Executor of this, my Last Will and Testament, to serve without bond or surety. In the event that he or she is unable or unwilling to serve at any time or for any reason then I nominate, constitute and appoint _____ as alternate Executor also to serve without bond or surety. I give my said Executor the fullest power in all matters including the power to sell or convey real or personal property or any interest therein without court order. My Executor shall serve as an independent executor, and no action shall be had in the county court in relation to the settlement of my estate other than the probating and recording of my Will and the return of an inventory, appraisement and list of claims of my estate, as provided by law.

IN WITNESS WHEREOF I declare this to be my Last Will and Testament and execute it willingly as my free and voluntary act for the purposes expressed herein and I am of legal age and sound mind and make this under no constraint or undue influence, this _____ day of _____, _____.

_____

The foregoing instrument was on said date subscribed at the end thereof by _____, the above named Testator who signed, published, and declared this instrument to be his/her Last Will and Testament in the presence of us and each of us, who thereupon at his/her request, in his/her presence, and in the presence of each other, have hereunto subscribed our names as witnesses thereto. We understand this to be his/her will and to the best of our knowledge testator is of legal age, of sound mind and under no constraint or undue influence.

_____residing at_____

_____residing at_____

Last Will and Testament

I, _____ a resident of _____ County, Texas do hereby make, publish and declare this to be my Last Will and Testament, hereby revoking any and all Wills and Codicils heretofore made by me.

FIRST: I direct that all my just debts and funeral expenses be paid out of my estate as soon after my death as is practicable.

SECOND: I give and bequeath the following personal property unto the following persons:

_____ to _____
_____ to _____
_____ to _____

THIRD: All the rest, residue and remainder of my estate, real or personal, whereso-ever situate, now owned or hereafter acquired by me, which at the time of my death shall belong to me or be subject to my disposal by will, I give, devise and bequeath unto my spouse, _____. If my said spouse does not survive me, I give, and bequeath the said property to my children _____ _____ _____,

plus any afterborn or adopted children in equal shares.

FOURTH: In the event that any beneficiary fails to survive me by thirty days, then this will shall take effect as if that person had predeceased me.

FIFTH: Should my spouse not survive me, I hereby nominate, constitute and appoint _____, as guardian over the person of any of my children who have not reached the age of majority at the time of my death. In the event that said guardian is unable or unwilling to serve then I nominate, constitute and appoint _____ _____ as guardian. Said guardian to serve without bond or surety.

SIXTH: Should my spouse not survive me, I hereby nominate, constitute and appoint _____ as guardian over the estate of any of my children who have not reached the age of majority at the time of my death. In the event that said guardian is unable or unwilling to serve then I nominate, constitute and appoint _____ _____ as guardian. Said guardian to serve without bond or surety.

SEVENTH: I hereby nominate, constitute and appoint _____ to serve as Executor of this, my Last Will and Testament, to serve without bond or surety. In the event that he or she is unable or unwilling to serve at any time or for any reason then I nominate, constitute and appoint _____ as alternate Executor also to serve without bond or surety. I give my said Executor the fullest power in all matters including the power to sell or convey real or personal property or any interest therein with-out court order. My Executor shall serve as an independent executor, and no action shall be had in the county court in relation to the settlement of my estate other than the probating and recording of my Will and the return of an inventory, appraisement and list of claims of my estate, as provided by law.

IN WITNESS WHEREOF I declare this to be my Last Will and Testament and execute it willingly as my free and voluntary act for the purposes expressed herein and I am of legal age and sound mind and make this under no constraint or undue influence, this _____ day of _____, _____.

_____

The foregoing instrument was on said date subscribed at the end thereof by _____, the above named Testator who signed, published, and declared this instrument to be his/her Last Will and Testament in the presence of us and each of us, who thereupon at his/her request, in his/her presence, and in the presence of each other, have hereunto subscribed our names as witnesses thereto. We understand this to be his/her will and to the best of our knowledge testator is of legal age, of sound mind and under no constraint or undue influence.

_____residing at_____

_____residing at_____

Last Will and Testament

I, _____ a resident of _____ County, Texas do hereby make, publish and declare this to be my Last Will and Testament, hereby revoking any and all Wills and Codicils heretofore made by me.

FIRST: I direct that all my just debts and funeral expenses be paid out of my estate as soon after my death as is practicable.

SECOND: I give and bequeath the following personal property unto the following persons:

_____ to _____
_____ to _____
_____ to _____

THIRD: All the rest, residue and remainder of my estate, real or personal, whereso-ever situate, now owned or hereafter acquired by me, which at the time of my death shall belong to me or be subject to my disposal by will, I give, devise and bequeath unto my spouse, _____. If my said spouse does not survive me, I give, and bequeath the said property to my children _____

_____

_____,

plus any afterborn or adopted children in equal shares.

FOURTH: In the event that any beneficiary fails to survive me by thirty days, then this will shall take effect as if that person had predeceased me.

FIFTH: In the event that any of my children have not reached the age of _____ years at the time of my death, then the share of any such child shall be held IN TRUST by _____until such time as such child or children reach the age of _____ years. The trustee shall use the income and that part of the principal of the trust as is, in the discretion of the trustee, necessary or desirable to provide proper housing, medical care, food, clothing, entertainment and education for the trust beneficiaries. In the event the said trustee is unable or unwilling to serve for any reason, then I nominate, consti-tute and appoint _____as alternate trustee. No bond shall be required of either trustee in any jurisdiction.

SIXTH: Should my spouse not survive me, I hereby nominate, constitute and appoint_____as guardian over the person and estate of any of my children who have not reached the age of majority at the time of my death. In the event that said guardian is unable or unwilling to serve then I nominate, constitute and appoint_____ as guardian.

SEVENTH: I hereby nominate, constitute and appoint _____ to serve as Executor of this, my Last Will and Testament, to serve without bond or surety. In the event that he or she is unable or unwilling to serve at any time or for any reason then I nominate, constitute and appoint _____ as alternate Executor also to serve without bond or surety. I give my said Executor the fullest power in all matters including the power to sell or convey real or personal property or any interest therein without court order. My Executor shall serve as an independent executor, and no action shall be had in the county court in relation to the settlement of my estate other than the probating and recording of my Will and the return of an inventory, appraisement and list of claims of my estate, as provided by law.

IN WITNESS WHEREOF I declare this to be my Last Will and Testament and execute it willingly as my free and voluntary act for the purposes expressed herein and I am of legal age and sound mind and make this under no constraint or undue influence, this _____ day of _____, _____.

_____

The foregoing instrument was on said date subscribed at the end thereof by _____, the above named Testator who signed, published, and declared this instrument to be his/her Last Will and Testament in the presence of us and each of us, who thereupon at his/her request, in his/her presence, and in the presence of each other, have hereunto subscribed our names as witnesses thereto. We understand this to be his/her will and to the best of our knowledge testator is of legal age, of sound mind and under no constraint or undue influence.

_____residing at_____

_____residing at_____

Last Will and Testament

I, _____ a resident of _____ County, Texas do hereby make, publish and declare this to be my Last Will and Testament, hereby revoking any and all Wills and Codicils heretofore made by me.

FIRST: I direct that all my just debts and funeral expenses be paid out of my estate as soon after my death as is practicable.

SECOND: I give and bequeath the following personal property unto the following persons:

_____ to _____
_____ to _____
_____ to _____

THIRD: All the rest, residue and remainder of my estate, real or personal, whereso-ever situate, now owned or hereafter acquired by me, which at the time of my death shall belong to me or be subject to my disposal by will, I give, devise and bequeath unto my spouse, _____. If my said spouse does not survive me, I give, and bequeath the said property to _____ _____ _____, or the survivor of them.

FOURTH: In the event that any beneficiary fails to survive me by thirty days, then this will shall take effect as if that person had predeceased me.

FIFTH: I hereby nominate, constitute and appoint _____ to serve as Executor of this, my Last Will and Testament, to serve without bond or surety. In the event that he or she is unable or unwilling to serve at any time or for any reason then I nominate, constitute and appoint _____ as alternate Executor also to serve without bond or surety. I give my said Executor the fullest power in all matters including the power to sell or convey real or personal property or any interest therein without court order. My Executor shall serve as an independent executor, and no action shall be had in the coun-ty court in relation to the settlement of my estate other than the probating and recording of my Will and the return of an inventory, appraisement and list of claims of my estate, as pro-vided by law.

IN WITNESS WHEREOF I declare this to be my Last Will and Testament and exe-cute it willingly as my free and voluntary act for the purposes expressed herein and I am of legal age and sound mind and make this under no constraint or undue influence, this day of _____, _____.

_____

The foregoing instrument was on said date subscribed at the end thereof by
_____, the above named Testator who signed, pub-
lished, and declared this instrument to be his/her Last Will and Testament in the presence
of us and each of us, who thereupon at his/her request, in his/her presence, and in the
presence of each other, have hereunto subscribed our names as witnesses thereto. We
understand this to be his/her will and to the best of our knowledge testator is of legal age,
of sound mind and under no constraint or undue influence.

_____residing at_____

_____residing at_____

Last Will and Testament

I, _____ a resident of _____ County, Texas do hereby make, publish and declare this to be my Last Will and Testament, hereby revoking any and all Wills and Codicils heretofore made by me.

FIRST: I direct that all my just debts and funeral expenses be paid out of my estate as soon after my death as is practicable.

SECOND: I give and bequeath the following personal property unto the following persons:

_____ to _____
_____ to _____
_____ to _____

THIRD: All the rest, residue and remainder of my estate, real or personal, wheresoever situate, now owned or hereafter acquired by me, which at the time of my death shall belong to me or be subject to my disposal by will, I give, devise and bequeath unto my spouse, _____. If my said spouse does not survive me, I give, and bequeath the said property to _____ _____ _____, or to their lineal descendants, per stirpes.

FOURTH: In the event that any beneficiary fails to survive me by thirty days, then this will shall take effect as if that person had predeceased me.

FIFTH: I hereby nominate, constitute and appoint _____ to serve as Executor of this, my Last Will and Testament, to serve without bond or surety. In the event that he or she is unable or unwilling to serve at any time or for any reason then I nominate, constitute and appoint _____ as alternate Executor also to serve without bond or surety. I give my said Executor the fullest power in all matters including the power to sell or convey real or personal property or any interest therein without court order. My Executor shall serve as an independent executor, and no action shall be had in the county court in relation to the settlement of my estate other than the probating and recording of my Will and the return of an inventory, appraisement and list of claims of my estate, as provided by law.

IN WITNESS WHEREOF I declare this to be my Last Will and Testament and execute it willingly as my free and voluntary act for the purposes expressed herein and I am of legal age and sound mind and make this under no constraint or undue influence, this _____ day of _____, _____.

_____

The foregoing instrument was on said date subscribed at the end thereof by
_____, the above named Testator who signed, published, and declared this instrument to be his/her Last Will and Testament in the presence of us and each of us, who thereupon at his/her request, in his/her presence, and in the presence of each other, have hereunto subscribed our names as witnesses thereto. We understand this to be his/her will and to the best of our knowledge testator is of legal age, of sound mind and under no constraint or undue influence.

_____residing at_____

_____residing at_____

Last Will and Testament

I, _____ a resident of _____ County, Texas do hereby make, publish and declare this to be my Last Will and Testament, hereby revoking any and all Wills and Codicils heretofore made by me.

FIRST: I direct that all my just debts and funeral expenses be paid out of my estate as soon after my death as is practicable.

SECOND: I give and bequeath the following personal property unto the following persons:

_____ to _____
_____ to _____
_____ to _____

THIRD: All the rest, residue and remainder of my estate, real or personal, whereso-ever situate, now owned or hereafter acquired by me, which at the time of my death shall belong to me or be subject to my disposal by will, I give, devise and bequeath unto my spouse, _____. If my said spouse does not survive me, I give, and bequeath the said property to my children _____ _____ _____,

in equal shares or to their lineal descendants, per stirpes.

FOURTH: In the event that any beneficiary fails to survive me by thirty days, then this will shall take effect as if that person had predeceased me.

FIFTH: I hereby nominate, constitute and appoint _____ to serve as Executor of this, my Last Will and Testament, to serve without bond or surety. In the event that he or she is unable or unwilling to serve at any time or for any reason then I nominate, constitute and appoint _____ as alternate Executor also to serve without bond or surety. I give my said Executor the fullest power in all matters including the power to sell or convey real or personal property or any interest therein without court order. My Executor shall serve as an independent executor, and no action shall be had in the coun-ty court in relation to the settlement of my estate other than the probating and recording of my Will and the return of an inventory, appraisement and list of claims of my estate, as pro-vided by law.

IN WITNESS WHEREOF I declare this to be my Last Will and Testament and exe-cute it willingly as my free and voluntary act for the purposes expressed herein and I am of legal age and sound mind and make this under no constraint or undue influence, this _____ day of _____, _____.

_____

The foregoing instrument was on said date subscribed at the end thereof by
_____, the above named Testator who signed, pub-
lished, and declared this instrument to be his/her Last Will and Testament in the presence of
us and each of us, who thereupon at his/her request, in his/her presence, and in the presence
of each other, have hereunto subscribed our names as witnesses thereto. We understand this
to be his/her will and to the best of our knowledge testator is of legal age, of sound mind and
under no constraint or undue influence.

_____residing at_____

_____residing at_____

Last Will and Testament

I, _____ a resident of _____ County, Texas do hereby make, publish and declare this to be my Last Will and Testament, hereby revoking any and all Wills and Codicils heretofore made by me.

FIRST: I direct that all my just debts and funeral expenses be paid out of my estate as soon after my death as is practicable.

SECOND: I give and bequeath the following personal property unto the following persons:

_____ to _____
_____ to _____
_____ to _____

THIRD: All the rest, residue and remainder of my estate, real or personal, whereso-ever situate, now owned or hereafter acquired by me, which at the time of my death shall belong to me or be subject to my disposal by will, I give, devise and bequeath as follows:

_____% to my spouse, _____ and

_____% to my children, _____

_____

_____,

in equal shares or to their lineal descendants per stirpes.

FOURTH: In the event that any beneficiary fails to survive me by thirty days, then this will shall take effect as if that person had predeceased me.

FIFTH: I hereby nominate, constitute and appoint _____ to serve as Executor of this, my Last Will and Testament, to serve without bond or surety. In the event that he or she is unable or unwilling to serve at any time or for any reason then I nominate, constitute and appoint _____ as alternate Executor also to serve without bond or surety. I give my said Executor the fullest power in all matters including the power to sell or convey real or personal property or any interest therein without court order. My Executor shall serve as an independent executor, and no action shall be had in the coun-ty court in relation to the settlement of my estate other than the probating and recording of my Will and the return of an inventory, appraisement and list of claims of my estate, as pro-vided by law.

IN WITNESS WHEREOF I declare this to be my Last Will and Testament and exe-cute it willingly as my free and voluntary act for the purposes expressed herein and I am of legal age and sound mind and make this under no constraint or undue influence, this _____ day of _____, _____.

_____

The foregoing instrument was on said date subscribed at the end thereof by
_____, the above named Testator who signed, published, and declared this instrument to be his/her Last Will and Testament in the presence of us and each of us, who thereupon at his/her request, in his/her presence, and in the presence of each other, have hereunto subscribed our names as witnesses thereto. We understand this to be his/her will and to the best of our knowledge testator is of legal age, of sound mind and under no constraint or undue influence.

_____residing at_____

_____residing at_____

Last Will and Testament

I, _____ a resident of _____ County, Texas do hereby make, publish and declare this to be my Last Will and Testament, hereby revoking any and all Wills and Codicils heretofore made by me.

FIRST: I direct that all my just debts and funeral expenses be paid out of my estate as soon after my death as is practicable.

SECOND: I give and bequeath the following personal property unto the following persons:

_____ to _____
_____ to _____
_____ to _____

THIRD: All the rest, residue and remainder of my estate, real or personal, whereso-ever situate, now owned or hereafter acquired by me, which at the time of my death shall belong to me or be subject to my disposal by will, I give, devise and bequeath unto my children _____

_____

_____,

plus any afterborn or adopted children in equal shares or to their lineal descendants per stirpes.

FOURTH: In the event that any beneficiary fails to survive me by thirty days, then this will shall take effect as if that person had predeceased me.

FIFTH: In the event any of my children have not attained the age of 18 years at the time of my death, I hereby nominate, constitute and appoint _____ _____ as guardian over the person and estate of any of my children who have not reached the age of majority at the time of my death. In the event that said guardian is unable or unwilling to serve then I nominate, constitute and appoint _____ _____ as guardian. Said guardian to serve without bond or surety.

SIXTH: I hereby nominate, constitute and appoint _____ to serve as Executor of this, my Last Will and Testament, to serve without bond or surety. In the event that he or she is unable or unwilling to serve at any time or for any reason then I nominate, constitute and appoint _____ as alternate Executor also to serve without bond or surety. I give my said Executor the fullest power in all matters including the power to sell or convey real or personal property or any interest therein without court order. My Executor shall serve as an independent executor, and no action shall be had in the county court in relation to the settlement of my estate other than the probating and recording of my Will and the return of an inventory, appraisement and list of claims of my estate, as provided by law.

IN WITNESS WHEREOF I declare this to be my Last Will and Testament and execute it willingly as my free and voluntary act for the purposes expressed herein and I am of legal age and sound mind and make this under no constraint or undue influence, this _____ day of _____, _____.

_____

The foregoing instrument was on said date subscribed at the end thereof by _____, the above named Testator who signed, published, and declared this instrument to be his/her Last Will and Testament in the presence of us and each of us, who thereupon at his/her request, in his/her presence, and in the presence of each other, have hereunto subscribed our names as witnesses thereto. We understand this to be his/her will and to the best of our knowledge testator is of legal age, of sound mind and under no constraint or undue influence.

_____residing at_____

_____residing at_____

Last Will and Testament

I, _____ a resident of _____ County, Texas do hereby make, publish and declare this to be my Last Will and Testament, hereby revoking any and all Wills and Codicils heretofore made by me.

FIRST: I direct that all my just debts and funeral expenses be paid out of my estate as soon after my death as is practicable.

SECOND: I give and bequeath the following personal property unto the following persons:

_____ to _____
_____ to _____
_____ to _____

THIRD: All the rest, residue and remainder of my estate, real or personal, wheresoever situate, now owned or hereafter acquired by me, which at the time of my death shall belong to me or be subject to my disposal by will, I give, devise and bequeath unto my children _____

_____

_____,

plus any afterborn or adopted children in equal shares or to their lineal descendants per stirpes.

FOURTH: In the event that any beneficiary fails to survive me by thirty days, then this will shall take effect as if that person had predeceased me.

FIFTH: In the event any of my children have not attained the age of 18 years at the time of my death, I hereby nominate, constitute and appoint _____ _____ as guardian over the person of any of my children who have not reached the age of majority at the time of my death. In the event that said guardian is unable or unwilling to serve then I nominate, constitute and appoint _____ _____ as guardian. Said guardian to serve without bond or surety.

SIXTH: In the event any of my children have not attained the age of 18 years at the time of my death, I hereby nominate, constitute and appoint _____ _____ as guardian over the estate of any of my children who have not reached the age of majority at the time of my death. In the event that said guardian is unable or unwilling to serve then I nominate, constitute and appoint _____ _____ as guardian. Said guardian to serve without bond or surety.

SEVENTH: I hereby nominate, constitute and appoint _____ to serve as Executor of this, my Last Will and Testament, to serve without bond or surety. In the event that he or she is unable or unwilling to serve at any time or for any reason then I nominate, constitute and appoint _____ as alternate Executor also to serve without bond or surety. I give my said Executor the fullest power in all matters including the power to sell or convey real or personal property or any interest therein without court order. My Executor shall serve as an independent executor, and no action shall be had in the county court in relation to the settlement of my estate other than the probating and recording of my Will and the return of an inventory, appraisement and list of claims of my estate, as provided by law.

IN WITNESS WHEREOF I declare this to be my Last Will and Testament and execute it willingly as my free and voluntary act for the purposes expressed herein and I am of legal age and sound mind and make this under no constraint or undue influence, this _____ day of _____, _____.

_____

The foregoing instrument was on said date subscribed at the end thereof by _____, the above named Testator who signed, published, and declared this instrument to be his/her Last Will and Testament in the presence of us and each of us, who thereupon at his/her request, in his/her presence, and in the presence of each other, have hereunto subscribed our names as witnesses thereto. We understand this to be his/her will and to the best of our knowledge testator is of legal age, of sound mind and under no constraint or undue influence.

_____residing at_____

_____residing at_____

Last Will and Testament

I, _____ a resident of _____ County, Texas do hereby make, publish and declare this to be my Last Will and Testament, hereby revoking any and all Wills and Codicils heretofore made by me.

FIRST: I direct that all my just debts and funeral expenses be paid out of my estate as soon after my death as is practicable.

SECOND: I give and bequeath the following personal property unto the following persons:

_____ to _____
_____ to _____
_____ to _____

THIRD: All the rest, residue and remainder of my estate, real or personal, wheresoever situate, now owned or hereafter acquired by me, which at the time of my death shall belong to me or be subject to my disposal by will, I give, devise and bequeath unto my children _____
_____
_____,
plus any afterborn or adopted children in equal shares or to their lineal descendants per stirpes.

FOURTH: In the event that any beneficiary fails to survive me by thirty days, then this will shall take effect as if that person had predeceased me.

FIFTH: In the event that any of my children have not reached the age of _____ years at the time of my death, then the share of any such child shall be held IN TRUST by _____until such time as such child or children reach the age of _____ years. The trustee shall use the income and that part of the principal of the trust as is, in the discretion of the trustee, necessary or desirable to provide proper housing, medical care, food, clothing, entertainment and education for the trust beneficiaries. In the event the said trustee is unable or unwilling to serve for any reason, then I nominate, constitute and appoint _____as alternate trustee. No bond shall be required of either trustee in any jurisdiction.

SIXTH: In the event any of my children have not attained the age of 18 years at the time of my death, I hereby nominate, constitute and appoint _____ _____ as guardian over the property of any of my children who have not reached the age of majority at the time of my death. In the event that said guardian is unable or unwilling to serve then I nominate, constitute and appoint _____ _____ as guardian. Said guardian to serve without bond or surety.

SEVENTH: I hereby nominate, constitute and appoint _____ to serve as Executor of this, my Last Will and Testament, to serve without bond or surety. In the event that he or she is unable or unwilling to serve at any time or for any reason then I nominate, constitute and appoint _____ as alternate Executor also to serve without bond or surety. I give my said Executor the fullest power in all matters including the power to sell or convey real or personal property or any interest therein without court order. My Executor shall serve as an independent executor, and no action shall be had in the county court in relation to the settlement of my estate other than the probating and recording of my Will and the return of an inventory, appraisement and list of claims of my estate, as provided by law.

IN WITNESS WHEREOF I declare this to be my Last Will and Testament and execute it willingly as my free and voluntary act for the purposes expressed herein and I am of legal age and sound mind and make this under no constraint or undue influence, this _____ day of _____, _____.

_____

The foregoing instrument was on said date subscribed at the end thereof by _____, the above named Testator who signed, published, and declared this instrument to be his/her Last Will and Testament in the presence of us and each of us, who thereupon at his/her request, in his/her presence, and in the presence of each other, have hereunto subscribed our names as witnesses thereto. We understand this to be his/her will and to the best of our knowledge testator is of legal age, of sound mind and under no constraint or undue influence.

_____residing at_____

_____residing at_____

Last Will and Testament

I, _____ a resident of _____ County, Texas do hereby make, publish and declare this to be my Last Will and Testament, hereby revoking any and all Wills and Codicils heretofore made by me.

FIRST: I direct that all my just debts and funeral expenses be paid out of my estate as soon after my death as is practicable.

SECOND: I give and bequeath the following personal property unto the following persons:

_____ to _____
_____ to _____
_____ to _____

THIRD: All the rest, residue and remainder of my estate, real or personal, wheresoever situate, now owned or hereafter acquired by me, which at the time of my death shall belong to me or be subject to my disposal by will, I give, devise and bequeath unto my children _____
_____
_____,
in equal shares, or their lineal descendants per stirpes.

FOURTH: In the event that any beneficiary fails to survive me by thirty days, then this will shall take effect as if that person had predeceased me.

FIFTH: I hereby nominate, constitute and appoint _____ to serve as Executor of this, my Last Will and Testament, to serve without bond or surety. In the event that he or she is unable or unwilling to serve at any time or for any reason then I nominate, constitute and appoint _____ as alternate Executor also to serve without bond or surety. I give my said Executor the fullest power in all matters including the power to sell or convey real or personal property or any interest therein without court order. My Executor shall serve as an independent executor, and no action shall be had in the county court in relation to the settlement of my estate other than the probating and recording of my Will and the return of an inventory, appraisement and list of claims of my estate, as provided by law.

IN WITNESS WHEREOF I declare this to be my Last Will and Testament and execute it willingly as my free and voluntary act for the purposes expressed herein and I am of legal age and sound mind and make this under no constraint or undue influence, this _____ day of _____, _____.

_____

The foregoing instrument was on said date subscribed at the end thereof by
_____, the above named Testator who signed, pub-
lished, and declared this instrument to be his/her Last Will and Testament in the presence of
us and each of us, who thereupon at his/her request, in his/her presence, and in the presence
of each other, have hereunto subscribed our names as witnesses thereto. We understand this
to be his/her will and to the best of our knowledge testator is of legal age, of sound mind and
under no constraint or undue influence.

_____residing at_____

_____residing at_____

Last Will and Testament

I, _____ a resident of _____ County, Texas do hereby make, publish and declare this to be my Last Will and Testament, hereby revoking any and all Wills and Codicils heretofore made by me.

FIRST: I direct that all my just debts and funeral expenses be paid out of my estate as soon after my death as is practicable.

SECOND: I give and bequeath the following personal property unto the following persons:

_____ to _____
_____ to _____
_____ to _____

THIRD: All the rest, residue and remainder of my estate, real or personal, wheresoever situate, now owned or hereafter acquired by me, which at the time of my death shall belong to me or be subject to my disposal by will, I give, devise and bequeath unto my children _____

_____

_____,

in equal shares, or their lineal descendants per capita.

FOURTH: In the event that any beneficiary fails to survive me by thirty days, then this will shall take effect as if that person had predeceased me.

FIFTH: I hereby nominate, constitute and appoint _____ to serve as Executor of this, my Last Will and Testament, to serve without bond or surety. In the event that he or she is unable or unwilling to serve at any time or for any reason then I nominate, constitute and appoint _____ as alternate Executor also to serve without bond or surety. I give my said Executor the fullest power in all matters including the power to sell or convey real or personal property or any interest therein without court order. My Executor shall serve as an independent executor, and no action shall be had in the county court in relation to the settlement of my estate other than the probating and recording of my Will and the return of an inventory, appraisement and list of claims of my estate, as provided by law.

IN WITNESS WHEREOF I declare this to be my Last Will and Testament and execute it willingly as my free and voluntary act for the purposes expressed herein and I am of legal age and sound mind and make this under no constraint or undue influence, this _____ day of _____, _____.

_____

The foregoing instrument was on said date subscribed at the end thereof by _____, the above named Testator who signed, published, and declared this instrument to be his/her Last Will and Testament in the presence of us and each of us, who thereupon at his/her request, in his/her presence, and in the presence of each other, have hereunto subscribed our names as witnesses thereto. We understand this to be his/her will and to the best of our knowledge testator is of legal age, of sound mind and under no constraint or undue influence.

_____ residing at _____

_____ residing at _____

Last Will and Testament

I, _____ a resident of _____ County, Texas do hereby make, publish and declare this to be my Last Will and Testament, hereby revoking any and all Wills and Codicils heretofore made by me.

FIRST: I direct that all my just debts and funeral expenses be paid out of my estate as soon after my death as is practicable.

SECOND: I give and bequeath the following personal property unto the following persons:

_____ to _____

_____ to _____

_____ to _____

THIRD: All the rest, residue and remainder of my estate, real or personal, whereso-ever situate, now owned or hereafter acquired by me, which at the time of my death shall belong to me or be subject to my disposal by will, I give, devise and bequeath unto the following: _____ _____ _____,

or to the survivor of them.

FOURTH: In the event that any beneficiary fails to survive me by thirty days, then this will shall take effect as if that person had predeceased me.

FIFTH: I hereby nominate, constitute and appoint _____ to serve as Executor of this, my Last Will and Testament, to serve without bond or surety. In the event that he or she is unable or unwilling to serve at any time or for any reason then I nominate, constitute and appoint _____ as alternate Executor also to serve without bond or surety. I give my said Executor the fullest power in all matters including the power to sell or convey real or personal property or any interest therein without court order. My Executor shall serve as an independent executor, and no action shall be had in the county court in relation to the settlement of my estate other than the probating and recording of my Will and the return of an inventory, appraisement and list of claims of my estate, as provided by law.

IN WITNESS WHEREOF I declare this to be my Last Will and Testament and execute it willingly as my free and voluntary act for the purposes expressed herein and I am of legal age and sound mind and make this under no constraint or undue influence, this _____ day of _____, _____.

_____

The foregoing instrument was on said date subscribed at the end thereof by
_____, the above named Testator who signed, published, and declared this instrument to be his/her Last Will and Testament in the presence of us and each of us, who thereupon at his/her request, in his/her presence, and in the presence of each other, have hereunto subscribed our names as witnesses thereto. We understand this to be his/her will and to the best of our knowledge testator is of legal age, of sound mind and under no constraint or undue influence.

_____residing at_____

_____residing at_____

Last Will and Testament

I, _____ a resident of _____ County, Texas do hereby make, publish and declare this to be my Last Will and Testament, hereby revoking any and all Wills and Codicils heretofore made by me.

FIRST: I direct that all my just debts and funeral expenses be paid out of my estate as soon after my death as is practicable.

SECOND: I give and bequeath the following personal property unto the following persons:

_____ to _____
_____ to _____
_____ to _____

THIRD: All the rest, residue and remainder of my estate, real or personal, wheresoever situate, now owned or hereafter acquired by me, which at the time of my death shall belong to me or be subject to my disposal by will, I give, devise and bequeath unto the following _____

_____

_____,

in equal shares, or their lineal descendants per stirpes.

FOURTH: In the event that any beneficiary fails to survive me by thirty days, then this will shall take effect as if that person had predeceased me.

FIFTH: I hereby nominate, constitute and appoint _____ to serve as Executor of this, my Last Will and Testament, to serve without bond or surety. In the event that he or she is unable or unwilling to serve at any time or for any reason then I nominate, constitute and appoint _____ as alternate Executor also to serve without bond or surety. I give my said Executor the fullest power in all matters including the power to sell or convey real or personal property or any interest therein without court order. My Executor shall serve as an independent executor, and no action shall be had in the county court in relation to the settlement of my estate other than the probating and recording of my Will and the return of an inventory, appraisement and list of claims of my estate, as provided by law.

IN WITNESS WHEREOF I declare this to be my Last Will and Testament and execute it willingly as my free and voluntary act for the purposes expressed herein and I am of legal age and sound mind and make this under no constraint or undue influence, this _____ day of _____, _____.

_____

The foregoing instrument was on said date subscribed at the end thereof by
_____, the above named Testator who signed, pub-
lished, and declared this instrument to be his/her Last Will and Testament in the presence of
us and each of us, who thereupon at his/her request, in his/her presence, and in the presence
of each other, have hereunto subscribed our names as witnesses thereto. We understand this
to be his/her will and to the best of our knowledge testator is of legal age, of sound mind and
under no constraint or undue influence.

_____residing at_____

_____residing at_____

Self-Proving Affidavit

STATE OF TEXAS   §
                                   §

COUNTY OF _____   §

       BEFORE ME, the undersigned authority, on this day personally appeared
_____, _____
and_____, known to me to be the Testator and the witnesses, respectively, whose names are subscribed to the annexed or foregoing instrument in their respective capacities; and all of said persons being by me duly sworn, the Testator declared to me and to the witnesses in my presence that said instrument is his/her Will, and that he/she had willingly made and executed it as his/her free act and deed for the purposes therein expressed; and the witnesses, each on his oath, stated to me in the presence and hearing of the Testator that the Testator had declared to them that said instrument is his/her Will, and that he/she executed same as such and wanted each of them to sign it as a witness; and upon their oaths each witness stated further that they did sign the same as witnesses in the presence of the Testator and at his/her request, that he/she was at that time eighteen (18) years of age or over and was of sound mind, and that each of the witnesses was then at least fourteen (14) years of age.

_____
TESTATOR

_____
WITNESS

_____
WITNESS

SUBSCRIBED AND ACKNOWLEDGED before me by _____,
the Testator and subscribed and sworn to before me by the above-named witnesses this
_____ day of _____, _____.

_____
Notary Public   [Print Name] _____
State of Texas
My Commission Expires: _____

This page intentionally left blank.

Codicil to the Will of
_____

I, _____, a resident of _____ County, Texas declare this to be the first codicil to my Last Will and Testament dated _____, _____.

      FIRST: I hereby revoke the clause of my Will which reads as follows: _____
_____
_____
_____

      SECOND: I hereby add following clause to my Will: _____
_____
_____
_____

      THIRD: In all other respects I hereby confirm and republish my Last Will and Testament dated _____, _____.

Date: _____   _____

We, the undersigned persons, of lawful age, have on this _____ day of _____, _____, at the request of _____, witnessed his/her signature to the foregoing First Codicil to Will in the presence of each of us; and we have, at the same time and in his/her presence and in the presence of each other, subscribed our names hereto as attesting witnesses.

_____ residing at: _____
                                                     _____

_____ residing at: _____
                                                     _____

SELF-PROVING AFFIDAVIT

STATE OF TEXAS   §
                                  §
COUNTY OF _____ §

      BEFORE ME, the undersigned authority, on this day personally appeared _____ _____, _____, and_____, known to me to be the Testator and the witnesses, respectively, whose names are subscribed to the annexed or foregoing instrument in their respective capacities; and all of said persons being by me duly sworn, the Testator declared to me and to the witnesses in my presence that said instrument is his/her First Codicil to Will, and that he/she had willingly made and executed it as his/her free act and deed for the purposes therein expressed; and the witnesses, each on his oath, stated to me in the presence and hearing of the Testator that the Testator had declared to them that said instrument is his/her First Codicil to Will, and that he/she executed same as such and wanted each of them to sign it as a witness; and upon their oaths each witness stated further that they did sign the same as witnesses in the presence of the Testator and at his/her request, that he/she was at that time eighteen (18) years of age or over and was of sound mind, and that each of the witnesses was then at least fourteen (14) years of age.

_____   _____
TESTATOR   WITNESS

                                          _____
                                          WITNESS

SUBSCRIBED AND ACKNOWLEDGED before me by _____, the Testator and subscribed and sworn to before me by the above-named witnesses this ____ day of_____, _____.

                                          _____
                                          Notary Public

This page intentionally left blank.

DIRECTIVE TO PHYSICIANS AND
FAMILY OR SURROGATES

This is an important legal document known as an Advance Directive. It is designed to help you communicate your wishes about medical treatment at some time in the future when you are unable to make your wishes known because of illness or injury. These wishes are usually based on personal values. In particular, you may want to consider what burdens or hardships of treatment you would be willing to accept for a particular amount of benefit obtained if you were seriously ill.

You are encouraged to discuss your values and wishes with your family or chosen spokesperson, as well as your physician. Your physician, other health care provider, or medical institution may provide you with various resources to assist you in completing your advance directive. Brief definitions are listed within the document and may aid you in your discussions and advance planning. Initial the treatment choices that best reflect your personal preferences. Provide a copy of your directive to your physician, usual hospital, and family or spokesperson. Consider a periodic review of this document. By periodic review, you can best assure that the directive reflects your preferences.

In addition to this advance directive, Texas law provides for two other types of directives that can be important during a serious illness. These are the Medical Power of Attorney and the Out-of-Hospital Do-Not-Resuscitate Order. You may wish to discuss these with your physician, family, hospital representative, or other advisers. You may also wish to complete a directive related to the donation of organs and tissues.

DEFINITIONS:

"Artificial nutrition and hydration" means the provision of nutrients or fluids by a tube inserted in a vein, under the skin in the subcutaneous tissues, or in the stomach (gastrointestinal tract).

"Irreversible condition" means a condition, injury, or illness: that may be treated, but is never cured or eliminated;that leaves a person unable to care for or make decisions for the person's own self; and that, without life-sustaining treatment provided in accordance with the prevailing standard of medical care, is fatal.

Explanation: Many serious illnesses such as cancer, failure of major organs (kidney, heart, liver, or lung), and serious brain disease such as Alzheimer's dementia may be considered irreversible early on. There is no cure, but the patient may be kept alive for prolonged periods of time if the patient receives life-sustaining treatments. Late in the course of the same illness, the disease may be considered terminal when, even with treatment, the patient is expected to die. You may wish to consider which burdens of treatment you would be willing to accept in an effort to achieve a particular outcome. This is a very personal decision that you may wish to discuss with your physician, family, or other important persons in your life.

"Life-sustaining treatment" means treatment that, based on reasonable medical judgment, sustains the life of a patient without which the patient will die. The term includes both life-sustaining medications and artificial life support such as mechanical breathing machines, kidney dialysis treatment, and artificial hydration and nutrition. The term does not include the administration of pain management medication, the performance of a medical procedure necessary to provide comfort care, or any other medical care provided to alleviate a patient's pain.

"Terminal condition" means an incurable condition caused by injury, disease, or illness that according to reasonable medical judgment will produce death within six months, even with available life-sustaining treatment provided in accordance with the prevailing standard of medical care.

Explanation: Many serious illnesses may be considered irreversible early in the course of the illness, but they may not be considered terminal until the disease is fairly advanced. In thinking about terminal illness and its treatment, you may wish to consider the relative benefits and burdens of treatment and discuss your wishes with your physician, family, or other important persons in your life.

ADVANCE DIRECTIVE

I,_____, recognize that the best health care is based upon a partnership of trust and communication with my physician. My physician and I will make health care decisions together as long as I am of sound mind and able to make my wishes known. If there comes a time that I am unable to make medical decisions about myself because of illness or injury, I direct that the following treatment preferences be honored:

If, in the judgment of my physician, I am suffering with a terminal condition from which I am expected to die within six months, even with available life-sustaining treatment provided in accordance with prevailing standards of medical care:

_____ I request that all treatments other than those needed to keep me comfortable be discontinued or withheld and my physician allow me to die as gently as possible; OR

_____ I request that I be kept alive in this terminal condition using available life-sustaining treatment. (THIS SELECTION DOES NOT APPLY TO HOSPICE CARE.)

If, in the judgment of my physician, I am suffering with an irreversible condition so that I cannot care for myself or make decisions for myself and am expected to die without life-sustaining treatment provided in accordance with prevailing standards of medical care:

_____ I request that all treatment other than those needed to keep me comfortable be discontinued or withheld and my physician allow me to die as gently as possible; OR

_____ I request that I be kept alive in this irreversible condition using available life-sustaining treatment. (THIS SELECTION DOES NOT APPLY TO HOSPICE CARE.)

Additional requests: (After discussion with your physician, you may wish to consider listing particular treatments in this space that you do or do not want in specific circumstances, such as artificial nutrition and fluids, intravenous antibiotics, etc. Be sure to state whether you do or do not want the particular treatment.)

After signing this directive, if my representative or I elect hospice care, I understand and agree that only those treatments needed to keep me comfortable would be provided and I would not be given available life-sustaining treatments.

If I do not have a Medical Power of Attorney, and I am unable to make my wishes known, I designate the following person(s) to make treatment decisions with my physician compatible with my personal values:

1.
2.

(If a Medical Power of Attorney has been executed, than an agent already has been named and you should not list additional names in this document.)

If the above persons are not available, or if I have not designated a spokesperson, I understand that a spokesperson will be chosen for me following standards specified in the laws of Texas. If, in the judgment of my physician, my death is imminent within minutes to hours, even with the use of all available medical treatment provided within the prevailing standard of care, I acknowledge that all treatments may be withheld or removed except those needed to maintain my comfort. I understand that under Texas law this directive has no effect if I have been diagnosed as pregnant. This directive will remain in effect until I revoke it. No other person may do so.

Signed this _____ day of_____, 20____, in _____, _____ County, Texas.

Print Name: _____

The witnesses acknowledge that the declarant signed this directive in their presence and that each of them is over the age of eighteen (18) years and competent to witness this document. The witness designated at "Witness 1" is: (1) not a person designated by the declarant to make a treatment decision for the declarant; (2) not related to the declarant by blood or marriage; (3) not entitled to any portion of the declarant's estate on declarant's death; (4) not a claimant against the estate of the declarant; (5) not the attending physician or employee of the attending physician of declarant; and (6) not an officer, director, partner, or business office employee of a health care facility in which the declarant is being cared for or of any parent organization of the health care facility. Furthermore, if "Witness 1" is an employee of a health care facility in which the declarant is a patient, such witness is not involved in providing direct patient care to the declarant.

_____
Witness 1
Address: _____
_____

_____
Witness 2
Address: _____
_____

INFORMATION CONCERNING THE
MEDICAL POWER OF ATTORNEY

THIS IS AN IMPORTANT LEGAL DOCUMENT. BEFORE SIGNING THIS DOCUMENT, YOU SHOULD KNOW THESE IMPORTANT FACTS:

Except to the extent you state otherwise, this document gives the person you name as your agent the authority to make any and all health care decisions for you in accordance with your wishes, including your religious and moral beliefs, when you are no longer capable of making them yourself. Because "health care" means any treatment, service, or procedure to maintain, diagnose, or treat your physical or mental condition, your agent has the power to make a broad range of health care decisions for you. Your agent may consent, refuse to consent, or withdraw consent to medical treatment and may make decisions about withdrawing or withholding life-sustaining treatment. Your agent may not consent to voluntary inpatient mental health services, convulsive treatment, psychosurgery, or abortion. A physician must comply with your agent's instructions or allow you to be transferred to another physician.

Your agent's authority begins when your doctor certifies that you lack the capacity to make health care decisions.

Your agent is obligated to follow your instructions when making decisions on your behalf. Unless you state otherwise, your agent has the same authority to make decisions about your health care as you would have had.

It is important that you discuss this document with your physician or other health care provider before you sign it to make sure that you understand the nature and range of decisions that may be made on your behalf. If you do not have a physician, you should talk with someone else who is knowledgeable about these issues and can answer your questions. You do not need a lawyer's assistance to complete this document, but if there is anything in this document that you do not understand, you should ask a lawyer to explain it to you.

The person you appoint as agent should be someone you know and trust. The person must be 18 years of age or older or a person under 18 years of age who has had the disabilities of minority removed. If you appoint your health or residential care provider (e.g., your physician or an employee of a home health agency, hospital, nursing home, or residential care home, other than a relative), that person has to choose between acting as your agent or as your health or residential care provider; the law does not permit a person to do both at the same time.

You should inform the person you appoint that you want the person to be your health care agent. You should discuss this document with your agent and your physician and give each a signed copy. You should indicate on the document itself the people and institutions who have signed copies. Your agent is not liable for health care decisions made in good faith on your behalf.

Even after you have signed this document, you have the right to make health care decisions for yourself as long as you are able to do so and treatment cannot be given to you or stopped over your objection. You have the right to revoke the authority granted to your agent by informing your agent or your health or residential care provider orally or in writing, or by your execution of a subsequent Medical Power of Attorney. Unless you state otherwise, your appointment of a spouse dissolves on divorce.

This document may not be changed or modified. If you want to make changes in the document, you must make an entirely new one.

You may wish to designate an alternate agent in the event that your agent is unwilling, unable, or ineligible to act as your agent. Any alternate agent you designate has the same authority to make health care decisions for you.

THIS POWER OF ATTORNEY IS NOT VALID UNLESS IT IS SIGNED IN THE PRESENCE OF TWO OR MORE COMPETENT ADULT WITNESSES. THE FOLLOWING PERSONS MAY NOT ACT AS ONE OF THE WITNESSES:

(1)   the person you have designed as your agent;

(2)   a person related to you by blood or marriage;

(3)   a person entitled to any part of your estate after your death under a will or codicil executed by you or by operation of law;

(4)   your attending physician;

(5)   an employee of your attending physician;

(6)   an employee of a health care facility in which you are a patient if the employee is providing direct patient care to you or is an officer, director, partner, or business office employee of the health care facility or of any parent organization of the health care facility; or

(7)   a person who, at the time this power of attorney is executed, has a claim against any part of your estate after your death.

MEDICAL POWER OF ATTORNEY
AND DESIGNATION OF HEALTH CARE AGENT

1.   **DESIGNATION OF HEALTH CARE AGENT**

I, _____, appoint:

Name: _____

Address: _____

               _____

Phone: _____

as my agent to make any and all health care decisions for me, except to the extent I state otherwise in this document. This Medical Power of Attorney takes effect if I become unable to make my own health care decisions and this fact is certified in writing by my physician.

LIMITATIONS ON THE DECISION MAKING AUTHORITY OF MY AGENT ARE AS FOLLOWS:

2.   **DESIGNATION OF ALTERNATE AGENT**

(You are not required to designate an alternate agent but you may do so. An alternate agent may make the same health care decisions as the designated agent if the designated agent is unable or unwilling to act as your agent. If the agent designated is your spouse, the designation is automatically revoked by law if your marriage is dissolved).

If the person designated as my agent is unable or unwilling to make health care decisions for me, I designate the following person to serve as my agent to make health care decisions for me as authorized by this document:

First Alternate Agent

Name: _____
Address: _____

               _____
Phone: _____

Second Alternate Agent

Name: _____
Address: _____

Phone: _____

An original of this document is kept at:

The following individuals or institutions have signed copies:

Name: _____
Address: _____
        _____
Phone: _____

Name: _____
Address: _____
        _____
Phone: _____

3. DURATION

I understand that this Medical Power of Attorney exists indefinitely from the date I execute this document unless I establish a shorter time or revoke the power of attorney. If I am unable to make health care decisions for myself when this power of attorney expires, the authority I have granted my agent continues to exist until the time I become able to make health care decisions for myself.

(IF APPLICABLE) This Medical Power of Attorney ends on the following date:

4. PRIOR DESIGNATIONS REVOKED

I revoke any prior Medical Power of Attorney.

5. ACKNOWLEDGMENT OF DISCLOSURE STATEMENT

I have been provided with a disclosure statement explaining the effect of this document. I have read and understand that information contained in the disclosure statement.

(YOU MUST DATE AND SIGN THIS POWER OF ATTORNEY.)

I sign my name to this Medical Power of Attorney on the _____ day of _____, 20_____, at _____, _____ County, Texas.

_____

Print Name: _____

STATEMENT AND SIGNATURE OF FIRST WITNESS:

I am not the person appointed as agent by this document. I am not related to the principal by blood or marriage. I would not be entitled to any portion of the principal's estate on the principal's death. I am not the attending physician of the principal or an employee of the attending physician. I have no claim against any portion of the principal's estate on the principal's death. Furthermore, if I am an employee of a health care facility in which the principal is a patient, I am not involved in providing direct patient care to the principal and am not an officer, director, partner, or business office employee of the health care facility or of any parent organization of the health care facility.

Witness Signature: _____

Print Name: _____ Date:_____

Address: _____

SIGNATURE OF SECOND WITNESS:

Witness Signature: _____

Print Name: _____ Date:_____

Address: _____

This page intentionally left blank.

DECLARATION OF GUARDIAN IN THE EVENT
OF LATER INCAPACITY OR NEED OF GUARDIAN

I, _____, make this Declaration of Guardian, to operate if the need for a guardian for me later arises.

1. I designate _____ to serve as a guardian of my person, _____ as first alternate guardian of my person, _____ as second alternate guardian of my person, and _____ as third alternate guardian of my person.

2. I designate _____ to serve as guardian of my estate, _____ as first alternate guardian of my estate, _____ as second alternate guardian of my estate, and _____ as third alternate guardian of my estate.

3. If any guardian or alternate guardian dies, does not qualify, or resigns, the next named alternate guardian becomes my guardian.

4. I expressly disqualify the following person(s) from serving as guardian of my person: _____.

5. I expressly disqualify the following person(s) from serving as guardian of my estate: _____.

SIGNED this _____ day of _____, 20_____.

Witness _____   Print Name: _____

Witness _____   Print Name: _____

SELF-PROVING AFFIDAVIT

STATE OF TEXAS   §
                            §

COUNTY OF _____ §

BEFORE ME, the undersigned authority, on this date personally appeared _____, _____ and _____, the declarant and witnesses, respectively, and all being duly sworn, the declarant said that the above instrument was his or her Declaration of Guardian and that the declarant had made and executed it for the purposes expressed in the declaration. The witnesses declared to me that they are each 14 years of age or older, that they saw the declarant sign the declaration, that they signed the declaration as witnesses, and that the declarant appeared to them to be of sound mind.

Declarant _____

Witness _____

Witness _____

SUBSCRIBED AND SWORN to before me by the above named declarant and witnesses on this the _____ day of _____, 20_____.

Name [print]:
Notary Public, State of Texas
My commission expires:

DECLARATION OF APPOINTMENT OF GUARDIAN
FOR MY CHILDREN IN THE EVENT OF MY DEATH OR INCAPACITY

I, _____, make this Declaration to appoint as guardian my child or children, listed herein, in the event of my death or incapacity:

Child: _____

Birthdate: _____

Child: _____

Birthdate: _____

I designate _____ to serve as guardian of the person of my (child or children), _____ as first alternate guardian of the person of my (child or children), _____ as second alternate guardian of the person of my (child or children), and _____ as third alternate guardian of the person of my (child or children).

I direct that the guardian of the person of my (child or children) serve (with or without) bond.

I designate _____ to serve as guardian of the estate of my (child or children), _____ as first alternate guardian of the estate of my (child or children), _____ as second alternate guardian of the estate of my (child or children), and _____ as third alternate guardian of the estate of my (child or children).

If any guardian or alternate guardian dies, does not qualify, or resigns the next named alternate guardian becomes guardian of my (child or children).

Signed this _____ day of _____, 20_____.

Declarant _____

Print Name: _____

Witness _____

Witness _____

SELF-PROVING AFFIDAVIT

STATE OF TEXAS   §
                            §

COUNTY OF _____   §

Before me, the undersigned authority, on this date personally appeared the declarant, _____, and   and as witnesses, and all being duly sworn, the declarant said that the above instrument was his or her Declaration of Appointment of Guardian for the Declarant's Children in the Event of Declarant's Death or Incapacity and that declarant had made and executed it for the purposes expressed in the declaration. The witnesses declared to me that they are each 14 years of age or older, that they saw the declarant sign the declaration, that they signed the declaration as witnesses, and that the declarant appeared to them to be of sound mind.

Declarant: _____

Witness: _____

Witness: _____

Subscribed and sworn to before me by the above named declarant and affiants on this _____ day of _____, 20_____.

Name (Print): _____
Notary Public, State of Texas
My commission expires:_____

UNIFORM DONOR CARD

The undersigned hereby makes this anatomical gift, if medically acceptable, to take effect on death. The words and marks below indicate my desires:

I give:

       (a) _____ any needed organs or parts;

       (b) _____ only the following organs or parts

_____

for the purpose of transplantation, therapy, medical research, or education;

       (c) _____ my body for anatomical study if needed.

Limitations or special wishes, if any:

_____

Signed by the donor and the following witnesses in the presence of each other:

_____   _____
Signature of Donor   Date of birth

_____   _____
Date signed   City & State

_____   _____
Witness   Witness

_____   _____
Address   Address

UNIFORM DONOR CARD

The undersigned hereby makes this anatomical gift, if medically acceptable, to take effect on death. The words and marks below indicate my desires:

I give:

       (a) _____ any needed organs or parts;

       (b) _____ only the following organs or parts

_____

for the purpose of transplantation, therapy, medical research, or education;

       (c) _____ my body for anatomical study if needed.

Limitations or special wishes, if any:

_____

Signed by the donor and the following witnesses in the presence of each other:

_____   _____
Signature of Donor   Date of birth

_____   _____
Date signed   City & State

_____   _____
Witness   Witness

_____   _____
Address   Address

UNIFORM DONOR CARD

The undersigned hereby makes this anatomical gift, if medically acceptable, to take effect on death. The words and marks below indicate my desires:

I give:

       (a) _____ any needed organs or parts;

       (b) _____ only the following organs or parts

_____

for the purpose of transplantation, therapy, medical research, or education;

       (c) _____ my body for anatomical study if needed.

Limitations or special wishes, if any:

_____

Signed by the donor and the following witnesses in the presence of each other:

_____   _____
Signature of Donor   Date of birth

_____   _____
Date signed   City & State

_____   _____
Witness   Witness

_____   _____
Address   Address

UNIFORM DONOR CARD

The undersigned hereby makes this anatomical gift, if medically acceptable, to take effect on death. The words and marks below indicate my desires:

I give:

       (a) _____ any needed organs or parts;

       (b) _____ only the following organs or parts

_____

for the purpose of transplantation, therapy, medical research, or education;

       (c) _____ my body for anatomical study if needed.

Limitations or special wishes, if any:

_____

Signed by the donor and the following witnesses in the presence of each other:

_____   _____
Signature of Donor   Date of birth

_____   _____
Date signed   City & State

_____   _____
Witness   Witness

_____   _____
Address   Address

One of these cards should be cut out and carried in your wallet or purse.

Index

Your #1 Source for Real World Legal Information...

SPHINX® PUBLISHING
An Imprint of Sourcebooks, Inc.®
- Written by lawyers
- Simple English explanation of the law
- Forms and instructions included

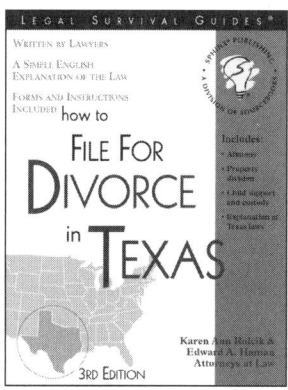  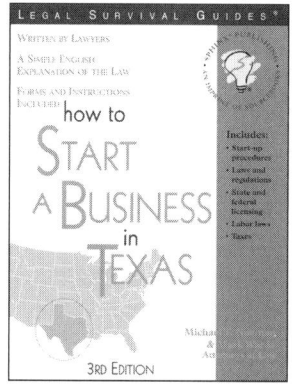

HOW TO FILE FOR DIVORCE IN TEXAS, 3RD ED.	**HOW TO WRITE YOUR OWN LIVING WILL, 2ND ED.**	**HOW TO START A BUSINESS IN TEXAS, 3RD ED.**

Step-by-step guide for filing for divorce in Texas with forms. Explains all aspects of divorce including child custody, child support, alimony, and what to do if you can't find your spouse. Why spend thousands of dollars when you can do it yourself?

256 pages; $24.95;
ISBN 1-57248-172-2

In a traumatic situation, the decision of life support could be very difficult for a family member to make. Make your wishes known ahead of time by using this step-by-step guide for writing living wills in all 50 states and the District of Columbia. Complete with necessary forms.

192 pages; $16.95;
ISBN 1-57248-118-8

Provides essential information on matters crucial to business success, such as licensing, name registration, and taxes.

264 pages; $18.95;
ISBN 1-57071-365-0

See the following order form for books written specifically for California, Florida, Georgia, Illinois, Massachusetts, Michigan, Minnesota, New York, North Carolina, Ohio, Pennsylvania, and Texas!

What our customers say about our books:

"It couldn't be more clear for the lay person." —R.D.

"I want you to know I really appreciate your book. It has saved me a lot of time and money." —L.T.

"Your real estate contracts book has saved me nearly $12,000.00 in closing costs over the past year." —A.B.

"...many of the legal questions that I have had over the years were answered clearly and concisely through your plain English interpretation of the law." —C.E.H.

"If there weren't people out there like you I'd be lost. You have the best books of this type out there." —S.B.

"...your forms and directions are easy to follow." —C.V.M.

Sphinx Publishing's Legal Survival Guides
are directly available from Sourcebooks, Inc., or from your local bookstores.
For credit card orders call 1–800–432–7444, write P.O. Box 4410, Naperville, IL 60567-4410,
or fax 630-961-2168
Find more legal information at: www.SphinxLegal.com

SPHINX® PUBLISHING'S NATIONAL TITLES
Valid in All 50 States

LEGAL SURVIVAL IN BUSINESS

The Complete Book of Corporate Forms	$24.95
How to Form a Limited Liability Company	$22.95
Incorporate in Delaware from Any State	$24.95
Incorporate in Nevada from Any State	$24.95
How to Form a Nonprofit Corporation (2E)	$24.95
How to Form Your Own Corporation (3E)	$24.95
How to Form Your Own Partnership (2E)	$24.95
How to Register Your Own Copyright (4E)	$24.95
How to Register Your Own Trademark (3E)	$21.95
Most Valuable Business Legal Forms You'll Ever Need (3E)	$21.95
The Small Business Owner's Guide to Bankruptcy	$21.95

LEGAL SURVIVAL IN COURT

Crime Victim's Guide to Justice (2E)	$21.95
Grandparents' Rights (3E)	$24.95
Help Your Lawyer Win Your Case (2E)	$14.95
Jurors' Rights (2E)	$12.95
Legal Research Made Easy (3E)	$21.95
Winning Your Personal Injury Claim (2E)	$24.95
Your Rights When You Owe Too Much	$16.95

LEGAL SURVIVAL IN REAL ESTATE

Essential Guide to Real Estate Contracts	$18.95
Essential Guide to Real Estate Leases	$18.95
How to Buy a Condominium or Townhome (2E)	$19.95

LEGAL SURVIVAL IN PERSONAL AFFAIRS

Cómo Hacer su Propio Testamento	$16.95
Cómo Solicitar su Propio Divorcio	$24.95
Cómo Restablecer su propio Crédito y Renegociar sus Deudas	$21.95
Guía de Inmigración a Estados Unidos (3E)	$24.95
Guía de Justicia para Víctimas del Crimen	$21.95
The 529 College Savings Plan	$16.95
How to File Your Own Bankruptcy (5E)	$21.95
How to File Your Own Divorce (4E)	$24.95
How to Make Your Own Simple Will (3E)	$18.95
How to Write Your Own Living Will (2E)	$16.95
How to Write Your Own Premarital Agreement (3E)	$24.95
Living Trusts and Other Ways to Avoid Probate (3E)	$24.95
Manual de Beneficios para el Seguro Social	$18.95
Mastering the MBE	$16.95
Most Valuable Personal Legal Forms You'll Ever Need	$24.95
Neighbor v. Neighbor (2E)	$16.95
The Nanny and Domestic Help Legal Kit	$22.95
The Power of Attorney Handbook (4E)	$19.95
Repair Your Own Credit and Deal with Debt	$18.95
The Social Security Benefits Handbook (3E)	$18.95
Social Security Q&A	$12.95
Sexual Harassment:Your Guide to Legal Action	$18.95
Teen Rights	$22.95
Unmarried Parents' Rights	$19.95
U.S. Immigration Step by Step	$21.95
U.S.A. Immigration Guide (4E)	$24.95
The Visitation Handbook	$18.95
Win Your Unemployment Compensation Claim (2E)	$21.95
Your Right to Child Custody, Visitation and Support (2E)	$24.95

Legal Survival Guides are directly available from Sourcebooks, Inc., or from your local bookstores.
Prices are subject to change without notice.

For credit card orders call 1–800–432–7444, write P.O. Box 4410, Naperville, IL 60567-4410
or fax 630-961-2168

Find more legal information at: www.SphinxLegal.com

SPHINX® PUBLISHING ORDER FORM

BILL TO:		SHIP TO:	
Phone #	Terms	F.O.B. Chicago, IL	Ship Date

Charge my: ☐ VISA   ☐ MasterCard   ☐ American Express

☐ **Money Order or Personal Check**

Credit Card Number [ ][ ][ ][ ][ ][ ][ ][ ][ ][ ][ ][ ][ ][ ][ ][ ]   Expiration Date

Qty	ISBN	Title	Retail	Ext.
		SPHINX PUBLISHING NATIONAL TITLES		
	1-57248-148-X	Cómo Hacer su Propio Testamento	$16.95	
	1-57248-147-1	Cómo Solicitar su Propio Divorcio	$24.95	
	1-57248-226-5	Cómo Restablecer su propio Crédito y Renegociar sus Deudas	$21.95	
	1-57248-238-9	The 529 College Savings Plan	$16.95	
	1-57248-166-8	The Complete Book of Corporate Forms	$24.95	
	1-57248-163-3	Crime Victim's Guide to Justice (2E)	$21.95	
	1-57248-159-5	Essential Guide to Real Estate Contracts	$18.95	
	1-57248-160-9	Essential Guide to Real Estate Leases	$18.95	
	1-57248-139-0	Grandparents' Rights (3E)	$24.95	
	1-57248-188-9	Guía de Inmigración a Estados Unidos (3E)	$24.95	
	1-57248-187-0	Guía de Justicia para Víctimas del Crimen	$21.95	
	1-57248-103-X	Help Your Lawyer Win Your Case (2E)	$14.95	
	1-57248-164-1	How to Buy a Condominium or Townhome (2E)	$19.95	
	1-57248-191-9	How to File Your Own Bankruptcy (5E)	$21.95	
	1-57248-132-3	How to File Your Own Divorce (4E)	$24.95	
	1-57248-083-1	How to Form a Limited Liability Company	$22.95	
	1-57248-231-1	How to Form a Nonprofit Corporation (2E)	$24.95	
	1-57248-133-1	How to Form Your Own Corporation (3E)	$24.95	
	1-57248-224-9	How to Form Your Own Partnership (2E)	$24.95	
	1-57248-232-X	How to Make Your Own Simple Will (3E)	$18.95	
	1-57248-200-1	How to Register Your Own Copyright (4E)	$24.95	
	1-57248-104-8	How to Register Your Own Trademark (3E)	$21.95	
	1-57248-118-8	How to Write Your Own Living Will (2E)	$16.95	
	1-57248-156-0	How to Write Your Own Premarital Agreement (3E)	$24.95	
	1-57248-230-3	Incorporate in Delaware from Any State	$24.95	
	1-57248-158-7	Incorporate in Nevada from Any State	$24.95	
	1-57071-333-2	Jurors' Rights (2E)	$12.95	
	1-57248-223-0	Legal Research Made Easy (3E)	$21.95	
	1-57248-165-X	Living Trusts and Other Ways to Avoid Probate (3E)	$24.95	
	1-57248-186-2	Manual de Beneficios para el Seguro Social	$18.95	

Qty	ISBN	Title	Retail	Ext.
	1-57248-220-6	Mastering the MBE	$16.95	
	1-57248-167-6	Most Valuable Bus. Legal Forms You'll Ever Need (3E)	$21.95	
	1-57248-130-7	Most Valuable Personal Legal Forms You'll Ever Need	$24.95	
	1-57248-098-X	The Nanny and Domestic Help Legal Kit	$22.95	
	1-57248-089-0	Neighbor v. Neighbor (2E)	$16.95	
	1-57248-169-2	The Power of Attorney Handbook (4E)	$19.95	
	1-57248-149-8	Repair Your Own Credit and Deal with Debt	$18.95	
	1-57248-217-6	Sexual Harassment: Your Guide to Legal Action	$18.95	
	1-57248-219-2	The Small Business Owner's Guide to Bankruptcy	$21.95	
	1-57248-168-4	The Social Security Benefits Handbook (3E)	$18.95	
	1-57248-216-8	Social Security Q&A	$12.95	
	1-57248-221-4	Teen Rights	$22.95	
	1-57071-399-5	Unmarried Parents' Rights	$19.95	
	1-57248-161-7	U.S.A. Immigration Guide (4E)	$24.95	
	1-57248-192-7	The Visitation Handbook	$18.95	
	1-57248-225-7	Win Your Unemployment Compensation Claim (2E)	$21.95	
	1-57248-138-2	Winning Your Personal Injury Claim (2E)	$24.95	
	1-57248-162-5	Your Right to Child Custody, Visitation and Support (2E)	$24.95	
	1-57248-157-9	Your Rights When You Owe Too Much	$16.95	
		CALIFORNIA TITLES		
	1-57248-150-1	CA Power of Attorney Handbook (2E)	$18.95	
	1-57248-151-X	How to File for Divorce in CA (3E)	$26.95	
	1-57071-356-1	How to Make a CA Will	$16.95	
	1-57248-145-5	How to Probate and Settle an Estate in California	$26.95	
	1-57248-146-3	How to Start a Business in CA	$18.95	
	1-57248-194-3	How to Win in Small Claims Court in CA (2E)	$18.95	
	1-57248-196-X	The Landlord's Legal Guide in CA	$24.95	
		FLORIDA TITLES		
	1-57071-363-4	Florida Power of Attorney Handbook (2E)	$16.95	
	1-57248-176-5	How to File for Divorce in FL (7E)	$26.95	
	1-57248-177-3	How to Form a Corporation in FL (5E)	$24.95	

To order, call Sourcebooks at 1-800-432-7444 or FAX (630) 961-2168 (Bookstores, libraries, wholesalers—please call for discount)

Prices are subject to change without notice.

Find more legal information at: www.SphinxLegal.com

SPHINX® PUBLISHING ORDER FORM

	Title	Retail	Ext.
	How to Form a Limited Liability Co. in FL (2E)	$24.95	_____
	How to Form a Partnership in FL	$22.95	_____
...ued on Following Page		**SUBTOTAL**	
_____ 1-57248-113-7	How to Make a FL Will (6E)	$16.95	_____
_____ 1-57248-088-2	How to Modify Your FL Divorce Judgment (4E)	$24.95	_____
_____ 1-57248-144-7	How to Probate and Settle an Estate in FL (4E)	$26.95	_____
_____ 1-57248-081-5	How to Start a Business in FL (5E)	$16.95	_____
_____ 1-57248-204-4	How to Win in Small Claims Court in FL (7E)	$18.95	_____
_____ 1-57248-202-8	Land Trusts in Florida (6E)	$29.95	_____
_____ 1-57248-123-4	Landlords' Rights and Duties in FL (8E)	$21.95	_____

GEORGIA TITLES

_____ 1-57248-137-4	How to File for Divorce in GA (4E)	$21.95	_____
_____ 1-57248-180-3	How to Make a GA Will (4E)	$21.95	_____
_____ 1-57248-140-4	How to Start a Business in Georgia (2E)	$16.95	_____

ILLINOIS TITLES

_____ 1-57248-206-0	How to File for Divorce in IL (3E)	$24.95	_____
_____ 1-57248-170-6	How to Make an IL Will (3E)	$16.95	_____
_____ 1-57248-247-8	How to Start a Business in IL (3E)	$21.95	_____
_____ 1-57248-078-5	Landlords' Rights & Duties in IL	$21.95	_____

MASSACHUSETTS TITLES

_____ 1-57248-128-5	How to File for Divorce in MA (3E)	$24.95	_____
_____ 1-57248-115-3	How to Form a Corporation in MA	$24.95	_____
_____ 1-57248-108-0	How to Make a MA Will (2E)	$16.95	_____
_____ 1-57248-106-4	How to Start a Business in MA (2E)	$18.95	_____
_____ 1-57248-209-5	The Landlord's Legal Guide in MA	$24.95	_____

MICHIGAN TITLES

_____ 1-57248-215-X	How to File for Divorce in MI (3E)	$24.95	_____
_____ 1-57248-182-X	How to Make a MI Will (3E)	$16.95	_____
_____ 1-57248-183-8	How to Start a Business in MI (3E)	$18.95	_____

MINNESOTA TITLES

_____ 1-57248-142-0	How to File for Divorce in MN	$21.95	_____
_____ 1-57248-179-X	How to Form a Corporation in MN	$24.95	_____
_____ 1-57248-178-1	How to Make a MN Will (2E)	$16.95	_____

NEW YORK TITLES

_____ 1-57248-193-5	Child Custody, Visitation and Support in NY	$26.95	_____
_____ 1-57248-141-2	How to File for Divorce in NY (2E)	$26.95	_____
_____ 1-57248-105-6	How to Form a Corporation in NY	$24.95	_____

Qty	ISBN	Title	Retail	Ext.
_____	1-57248-095-5	How to Make a NY Will (2E)	$16.95	_____
_____	1-57248-199-4	How to Start a Business in NY (2E)	$18.95	_____
_____	1-57248-198-6	How to Win in Small Claims Court in NY (2E)	$18.95	_____
_____	1-57248-197-8	Landlords' Legal Guide in NY	$24.95	_____
_____	1-57071-188-7	New York Power of Attorney Handbook	$19.95	_____
_____	1-57248-122-6	Tenants' Rights in NY	$21.95	_____

NORTH CAROLINA TITLES

_____	1-57248-185-4	How to File for Divorce in NC (3E)	$22.95	_____
_____	1-57248-129-3	How to Make a NC Will (3E)	$16.95	_____
_____	1-57248-184-6	How to Start a Business in NC (3E)	$18.95	_____
_____	1-57248-091-2	Landlords' Rights & Duties in NC	$21.95	_____

OHIO TITLES

_____	1-57248-190-0	How to File for Divorce in OH (2E)	$24.95	_____
_____	1-57248-174-9	How to Form a Corporation in OH	$24.95	_____
_____	1-57248-173-0	How to Make an OH Will	$16.95	_____

PENNSYLVANIA TITLES

_____	1-57248-242-7	Child Custody, Visitation and Support in Pennsylvania	$26.95	_____
_____	1-57248-211-7	How to File for Divorce in PA (3E)	$26.95	_____
_____	1-57248-094-7	How to Make a PA Will (2E)	$16.95	_____
_____	1-57248-112-9	How to Start a Business in PA (2E)	$18.95	_____
_____	1-57071-179-8	Landlords' Rights and Duties in PA	$19.95	_____

TEXAS TITLES

_____	1-57248-171-4	Child Custody, Visitation, and Support in TX	$22.95	_____
_____	1-57248-172-2	How to File for Divorce in TX (3E)	$24.95	_____
_____	1-57248-114-5	How to Form a Corporation in TX (2E)	$24.95	_____
_____	1-57248-255-9	How to Make a TX Will (3E)	$16.95	_____
_____	1-57248-214-1	How to Probate and Settle an Estate in TX (3E)	$26.95	_____
_____	1-57248-228-1	How to Start a Business in TX (3E)	$18.95	_____
_____	1-57248-111-0	How to Win in Small Claims Court in TX (2E)	$16.95	_____
_____	1-57248-110-2	Landlords' Rights and Duties in TX (2E)	$21.95	_____

SUBTOTAL THIS PAGE _____

SUBTOTAL PREVIOUS PAGE _____

Shipping — $5.00 for 1st book, $1.00 each additional _____

Illinois residents add 6.75% sales tax _____

Connecticut residents add 6.00% sales tax _____

TOTAL _____

To order, call Sourcebooks at 1-800-432-7444 or FAX (630) 961-2168 (Bookstores, libraries, wholesalers—please call for discount)
Prices are subject to change without notice.
Find more legal information at: www.SphinxLegal.com